PORTRAIT OF THE ARTIST AS AMERICAN

PORTRAIT OF THE ARTIST AS AMERICAN

BY MATTHEW JOSEPHSON

I feel I am an exile here. – HERMAN MELVILLE

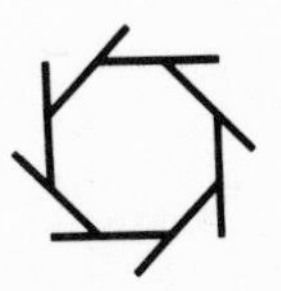

1964
OCTAGON BOOKS, INC.
NEW YORK

Reprinted 1964
by special arrangement with Matthew Josephson

OCTAGON BOOKS, INC.
175 FIFTH AVENUE
NEW YORK, N. Y. 10010

LIBRARY OF CONGRESS CATALOG CARD NUMBER: 64-24840

Printed in U.S.A. by
NOBLE OFFSET PRINTERS, INC.
NEW YORK 3, N. Y.

To H. J.

CONTENTS

Introduction: The Artist as American	ix
I. Libertarians and Others	3
II. The Belated Revelers	44
III. The Education of Henry James	70
IV. A 'Passionate Pilgrim'	98
V. Those Who Stayed	139
VI. An Enemy of the West: Lafcadio Hearn	199
VII. The Voyage of Stephen Crane	232
VIII. The Return of Henry James	265
IX. Excursion: The American Scene	289

Introduction

THE ARTIST AS AMERICAN

AS THE twentieth century grows older and unfolds its strange version of human life, cruel, absorbing, vertiginous, with its immense new zones, dimensions, powers, there are moments, nevertheless, when those of us who have retained the faculty for listening to our emotions or taking inventory of our ideas and days, suffer painful awakenings and the sense of formidable deficits felt and known. In these rare moods of reflection, we grow conscious of having come to live, mysteriously enough, within a mechanized, unfeeling order. The immediate world about us is pretty thoroughly regulated against individual outbursts of passion or eccentricity. We reside with our families in barracks; our work-rooms are boxes contained within greater boxes. Electric signals open and shut the public thoroughfares as effectually as if invisible bridges were momently lowered and raised above a deadly torrent. These are streets intended presumably for neither man nor beast, while great trees die along their border.

Modern man lives under the sign of the Machine, we tend to say. In reality there is nothing wrong with the Machine in itself; it is the morale or the mentality that speaks through it, commands through it, that is wrong: a mentality that is so sightless, so wanting in either program or objective for human character, that makes such meager provisions for the extra-physical *element in men, that they have the natural illusion of facing the Machine alone, as the one implacable condition that must be met. All our ruthlessly applied science, all our mechanism, is simply the offspring of the mind, the extension of human force and ingenuity. But the suspicion grows that the child, beyond control, now menaces the parent. . . .*

The commonest daily events suggest to us how completely human beings now live in masses, how they are directed to the time of machines, and how violently their natural emotions are altered or stamped out. Perhaps it will soon be hard to trace the resemblance between the new man and the traditional, historical—especially the sanguine and idealistic—notion of humanity. Certainly, to be merry and lively in the manner of older societies, such as that described by Trollope in England, seems something preposterous. Drinking, the most amiable of human indulgences, so conducive to amorousness, jocundity, or simply sweetness of humor, and encouraging the return to natural character (as proved by so many classical maxims), is publicly condemned.

In America, change has swept against no barriers

of tradition or religion, no lack of space or natural wealth. More rigidly than elsewhere, the energized mass is regimented and caught within an automatism: here the 'Machine Age' is known in full stride, with its miracles of convenience, its picturesqueness, its great alterations of folkways. And yet misgivings are voiced frequently enough in many quarters. We stare disconsolately at a picture of progress which is blemished by puzzling omens of 'diminishing returns.'

But if the natural emotions of the essentially unconcerned, rough and ready man-in-the-street are to be so drastically changed, to be made so anonymous, so automatic—what becomes then, as M. Paul Valéry has asked in a great pamphlet, of the 'higher man,' the man of sensibility, taste, disinterestedness, whose subtle or remotely meditative nature has been so fruitful in the long run for the human race?

There is, for instance, the dilemma of the artist in the modern world. No problem seems more fascinating than that of the destiny of the artist under the new order, a destiny which appeals to us more and more as something like fatal obliteration. In the United States one of the most striking events, underneath the prosperous surface of things, has been the emigration of talent to countries of an older civilization where some quantum of individual liberty is still to be enjoyed—or even to regions of a primitive cul-

ture where liberty is embraced to the exclusion of all other advantages.

For any defense of the apparently threatened humanities the case of the artist offers a short cut, a convenient symbol. In him we may see the human faculties, as against the animal or automatic appetites, at their apex: human intensity stated in its highest terms, as Henry Adams would say. In his proper medium he suggests always the sense of liberty, of free experiment, and of being capable of offering constant surprise, as against the type at the opposite extreme, in whom all the graces, the tricks of human fantasy, have been stamped out, who seems imprisoned within a routine; who, though holding the lever of machines or systems, may better be said to be held by them. Thus the dilemma of the artist under mechanism sums up that of a whole (formerly) independent class, all those who have been detached from the spirit of immediate gain, all who have had the sense of being disinterested—all the prophets, historians, philosophers, pure scientists who have served man so well by their frequent flights from the so-called Practical Realities.

The artist, then, appears most vulnerable. In a society become increasingly collective and uniform in its interests, no place has been left for his lonely and personal labor. With such a world, art in the older sense can no longer co-exist. The creative effort, thus far, has never been mechanical; it has never lent itself to mass-production. It has never even been practical, for, reluctant to use the organs of groups or to live in the spirit of masses, the artist has simply continued his sublimated play, his making of uselessly exquisite or magnificent things; he has continued to pursue, to solicit, values in an age given to mob distractions and all those passive amusements which are universal substitutes for thought.

Under mechanism, the eternal drama for the artist becomes resistance to the milieu, *as if the highest prerogative were the preservation of the individual type, the defense of the human self from dissolution in the horde.*

And yet no such misfortune appears to have befallen generally the great men of earlier periods; their lot was not cast with a desperate minority. Nor were they compelled to bid good-by to an implacable Wisconsin or New England and seek an exotic development in foreign lands. As one recalls the golden ages, the masters made their temples and cathedrals, their dramas and paintings, while living in harmony, for the most part, with their contemporary world.

If in our reflections on present dilemmas we glance back at a recent, an immediate past, we see in the earlier period of the young republic, and toward the middle of the nineteenth century, a phase of social upheaval of which our own cycle is the rigid se-

quence. The amazing realities of this period have long been shielded from us under the fustian of a vague Protestant shame. But time has laid aside all the glozing farrago which has served for our national history; we are no longer so confused as to what the past was or what was 'representative' in the past. And now, under our revised judgments, the experience of earlier generations offers many surprises and the utmost instruction.

The very possibility of civilization here seems to have been questioned passionately. The native literature, for instance, instead of being oblivious and compliant, appears full of the deepest presentiments, given to admonition and revolt, even a general burning of bridges. And it strikes us how precarious, how untenable, despite all effort, the foothold of art has always been in America, how in this limited, but vital sense there has always been a divided camp. . . .

One goes back, then, to the older artists for light on our present character and our present situation, much as we seek an understanding of a modern locomotive in the 'iron horse' of 1840.

Long, long, it seems, the dangers had been perceived of an unstable democracy, of herd-life, of the unbridled passion for gain, of the decline in the human and political arts. The defection from the crowd of early thinkers, the isolation or flight of earlier artists, seem precisely like that of our own time.

Did not Emerson exult over the panic of 1837! Men had become money-chests, the 'servants of their bellies'; he had seen 'the cruel oppression of the ideal' by the actual, so that 'the head served the feet.' And now—'Pride, and Expediency, who jeered and chirped and were so well pleased with themselves, and made merry with the dream, as they termed it, of Philosophy and Love—behold they are all flat, and here is the Soul erect and unconquered still.'

There was Thoreau, later, who said: 'Let your life be a counter-friction to stop the machine! . . . My thoughts are murder to the state and involuntarily go plotting against her.'

But the whole bright New England revival of the 1840's and 1850's, as we have learned, duplicates simply the libertarianism of eighteenth century France. It flourished for a time, with its unfrocked preachers, its moral originality, its lecture-institutes, its optimism and 'perfectionism'—so long as the States composed an agrarian nation, living still in the eighteenth century. Then the notion that man was essentially good, divine, free, so ardently defended, vanished in the thunder and cloud of the great Civil War.

It is at the hour of the Civil War that we find an intellectual crisis analogous to our own. There is ushered in an industrial revolution which, for all its tardiness, moves with giant bounds to encompass the whole continent, while social customs dissolve, regions lose their identity, fortunes change hands, and all the frontiers melt before the impact of an insatiable expansion.

In those days a fatality hung over the generation that came to manhood. They saw how peace brought its special horrors; steam-power and railroads in their careless youth functioned with a quite primitive brutality. They saw all recognizable landmarks swept away by the new economy. The more imaginative of the young men, who had been educated to literary and political tastes, viewed with dismay the scenes of scarred barrenness of 'anarchy-plus-the-police,' and could make nothing of it. They had the conviction that they belonged to another century or another climate; that they had been born too soon, or perhaps too late.

It is a distinguished generation, if we make allowance for the hostile conditions they faced. Certainly there is no lack of talent and initiated passion. After we have pruned away the débris of provisory reputations the names that remain, of Emily Dickinson and Henry James, of Ambrose Bierce, Lafcadio Hearn, and Stephen Crane, suggest a slender but genuine contribution to culture. Their work is discordant; it is limited, and, save for James, fatally brief. To these, the personalities of the spectacular

Whistler and the enigmatic Henry Adams are related; while the older men, Herman Melville and Walt Whitman, figure in their company as strange survivors almost to the end of the century.

How different is the note and scale of their work from that Promethean and heaven-defying one which had been awaited in a young nation of 'incalculable potentialities'! The whole group acquires, in the air of the greatly misunderstood period, a common attitude of melancholy dissent. It is aware of its questionable position in the social body; it is aware of the indifference of its audience, and in short, as Howells said, of being tolerated at best, rather than accepted.

'We're the disinherited of art!' wrote Henry James in his youth, persuaded that the whole native heritage was a dreadful handicap. 'We're excluded from the magic circle! The soil of American perception is a poor little barren artificial deposit. . . . We have neither taste nor force. How should we have them? Our crude and garish climate, our silent past, our deafening present, the constant pressure about us of unlovely conditions . . .'

Again and again we come upon the note of complaint and estrangement. 'Carpets, pianos, brass-bands, churches, how I hate them!' wrote Lafcadio Hearn in his letters; and he bristles with scorn of 'all that was energetic, swift,—all competition, rivalry, all striving in the race for success.'

In a large measure the strain of morbidity in Hawthorne and Poe seems to have been handed on. The obsession with evil, early sorrow and death, appears astonishingly native to the American muse, which often continues, during the later period, to live by preference in the enchanted and supernatural air of Arthur Gordon Pym—as if in an effort to escape from hateful realities. 'Whatever the American men of genius are,' an English critic observed, 'they are not young gods making a young world.'

If we examine the private writings and utterances of these older artists we find in most of them a consistent hatred and suspicion of democracy. Whether by implication or with bluntness, one after another indicated mistrust of the loose equalitarian social system, in which masses in an unceasing uproar thrust themselves toward physical gratification and power. This aspect of their dissent, the conflict between the motives of the artists and the will of the people, seems to touch the very root of the trouble.

The whole question whether the arts, in their historical character, can survive in democratic societies must be thrown open. One admits promptly that the artists were not looking at a pure democracy. But what revolution, what human cataclysm, ever led to perfect liberty or perfect equality? We know only the quasi-democracies of our experience, of our his-

tory. And it is here I think that liberal critics, such as Mr. Van Wyck Brooks and Mr. Lewis Mumford, have erred in attributing the defeat of American culture to the lack of true political liberties, the want of equality, the absence in short of 'the good life.' Here one sees also the fallacies of the libertarian Whitman, who sought to 'breathe a soul into the democracy.' With waning faith in the goodness of man (certainly, in the mass), we turn rather to the belief that it was the abundance of liberty, the universal equality of condition and motive, that may have been most fatal. Invariably the rights of man were preëmpted by the more aggressive and ruthless individuals of the Gilded Age while the spirit of equality led to a dreadful sameness of character.

In the turmoil of democracies, Tocqueville commented during his visit to early America, what flourishes most is trade. The masses instinctively follow their bolder members—the Goulds, Hills, Vanderbilts, who were the true heroes of the age—toward labor and plenty. These immigrants, these former peasants, remember only, by some effect of atavism, how hungry and naked men have largely been through the centuries. To their minds, every new method which leads by a shorter road to wealth, every machine which spares labor, diminishes the cost of production, facilitates or augments pleasure, seems the grandest effort of the human intellect. And so they asked nothing, Tocqueville noted as far back as 1840, of ideas, of the arts, of science, but their useful application toward ends of comfort and profit.

The sad artists of the Gilded Age, that is, those who were not lost in 'countless masses of adjustments,' longed for a stable social system, for an interesting variety of manners, forms, values. But the spectacle of Washington, for instance, in the '70s and '80s, disheartened them profoundly, as one perceives in the autobiography of Henry Adams. They would have sacrificed equality for the sake of some authority which could end the permanent earthquake conditions! Such an attitude, one recognizes, was greatly opposed to the will of the people. During the later nineteenth century immense numbers of human beings had risen for the first time to a much higher state of physical dignity than they had ever known. They would not relinquish these advantages, no matter what the spiritual or intangible cost. And the more one ponders on this phase of the muffled conflict between the luckless American aesthetes and their 'young world,' the more one is convinced that here was the principle in operation which determined the banishment, the extinction of their type and culture. Ill adjusted and isolated, their revolt took the form of flight: inwardly, a withdrawal into themselves; or outwardly, a physical expatriation. The generation which followed the Civil War deemed itself exiled:

and most often when it could no longer suffer obscurity and a kind of ostracism in the native environment, it fled abroad to a more favoring air.

How can we ignore the implications of their baffled lives? There is the obscure tragedy of Melville, a genius who passed half his life in silence as a clerk in the customs office of New York. Doomed, uncomprehending, hating the age, he wandered in the anonymous crowd, resigned to his disappearance from the world; he is a sphinx-like figure, living for thirty years in a tomb. And there are all the other ill-starred careers: James Whistler dies in London; Lafcadio Hearn in Japan; Stephen Crane meets death in Germany, early in life; Ambrose Bierce, as an old man, is killed by guerillas in Mexico; Henry James seeks to obliterate his origin in a long London life and becomes a British citizen in the days of the World War; Henry Adams, in despair of all else, haunts the Gothic cathedrals of France, worshiping the beauty and the logic of medieval art. The record is long and convincing; and there are many less salient cases. Was it not a young American, Henry Harland, who went to London in the '90s to found The Yellow Book? *There was Stuart Merrill, who discarded his own language for the French, to become one of the most esteemed of the Symbolist poets. There was the host of painters who found no sustenance at home, while success, as in the case of*

Abbey, Whistler, and so many others, awaited them abroad. There were middling novelists like Frederic and Marion Crawford, who vowed never, never to return to their native land, from Italy or Chelsea or wherever.

It is simply an exodus, a general expulsion of the civilized type—whether deliberate or unconscious, it matters little—from a country which above all needed ornament and civilization. For thirty or forty years migrations arose of starved artists, singly or in groups, toward Italy, France or England, which were seen as golden lands in whose favored climate art could be 'gathered in clusters.'

Of those who remained at home, living in such seclusion as Melville and Whitman found, Emily Dickinson seems one of the most curious and expressive figures. All her life long she concealed her strange poems, and of the paternal home and garden in Amherst she made a nunnery, living there only with God and scarcely stirring abroad to peep at the inconceivable and vain bustle outside. She scarcely stirred beyond her hedges—but when she did she could make pointed comments in her beautiful letters which illuminate the whole issue for us.

'How do most people live without thoughts?' she exclaims.

The very question is startling; and reveals more

than anything else the malaise of the exiles both within and without.

'There are many people in the world,' Emily Dickinson continues with her wild intuition. 'You must have noticed them in the street—how do they live? How do they get strength to put on their clothes in the morning? . . .'

PORTRAIT OF THE ARTIST AS AMERICAN

I

LIBERTARIANS AND OTHERS

They are all religious, but hate the churches; they reject the ways of living of other men, but have none to offer in their stead. Perhaps, one of these days, a great Yankee shall come who will easily do the unknown deed.—EMERSON TO CARLYLE.

IN THE revival of learning that took place during the early nineteenth century, it was New England that enjoyed authority and exercised leadership over the American States to a degree which we can scarcely understand nowadays. New England, then, offers a point of departure for our speculations on the darker periods that follow. With little exaggeration, we may see the whole rise and fall of a completed, native culture as drama—drama characterized by human figures and episodes, sometimes tenderly absurd in their excesses, sometimes tragic in their defeat.

Up to the chasm of the Civil War aspirants still looked toward Boston as a literary 'Holy Land'; Concord, the mellow, sleepy village near by, was a new 'northern Athens.' In 1860, William Dean Howells, as a young man, arriving from the hinterland of Ohio, was dazzled by meeting for the first time the great New England group. He was received by the Massachusetts patricians, 'gentlemen' like Edmund Quincy, and Francis Parkman, who despite their wealth and position engaged in no commerce, but devoted themselves wholly to letters and the improvement of their minds! In the Salem of Hawthorne he saw an ancient New England town and felt for the first time that which so many wandering Americans were later to seek in Europe: the power of long-rooted traditions, customs, of local gods, rising before him. With Dr. Oliver Wendell Holmes and Mr. James Fields, the editor of the famous *Atlantic*, he breakfasted in the high spacious rooms of one of the great houses overlooking the Charles River. The conversation scintillated as the two Brahmins sought to place the young poet at his ease. And suddenly, when they recalled that Howells was to join the great magazine, then Boston's pride and her *Revue des Deux Mondes*, the fancy had occurred to them of 'laying on hands,' thus humorously signalizing an apostolic succession which he, the raw Western youth, was to carry on.

After many years, Howells, worldly, cultivated, admired, became almost a converted New Englander; he exercised his own charming, decorous influence. But something was profoundly altered. A régime had ended. And a distinguished Bostonian, the late Mr. Barrett Wendell, has not failed to call attention to the portents so clearly indicated in this passing of literary power from the hands of natives of New England (and above all, graduates of Harvard), to those of a Westerner who, for all his admitted talents and sympathies, would never be able to understand truly the ways, the spirit and the genius of the people of Massachusetts Bay.

In New England's heroic age, some twenty years earlier—for 1860 was already comparatively late in her career—a swarm of prophets and Jeremiahs wandered down the roads near Boston, with long gowns and longer hair: Dunkers, Agrarians, Abolitionists, Vegetarians, Groaners, Come-outers, Swedenborgians, Mesmerists, Communists.

'What a fertility of projects for the salvation of the world!' Emerson had exclaimed good-humoredly.

Beneath the uncouth, discordant manifestations, all the fashions of dissent, there was nevertheless a strong current of ideas, resembling on a smaller scale that of France in the late eighteenth century. By a different route, and with the additional flourishes of their heredity, the New England thinkers had arrived at the same romantic exaltation of the ego, the same suspicion of society as the factor which corrupted natural man, the same worship of nature, the identical libertarianism of the age of Rousseau.

The local thinkers, however, diverged, in their idealistic or 'transcendental' emphasis. Their theory was opposed to materialism. They had as their New England heritage an originality which had always been theological and moral since Cotton Mather and Jonathan Edwards. But in the descent of great preachers men like Channing had arisen lately who could not endure the spirit of the Lord's vengeance, who renounced Original Sin. From the early upheavals of Unitarianism it had been but a step to the deism of Emerson, George Ripley and Theodore Parker. They had defrocked themselves and left their congregations—all religious, and hating the churches.

The Transcendentalists—as the men of the Concord School called themselves—had as their ruling idea a faith in man's goodness and perfectibility. Humanity was no longer debased, the creature of sin; it was divine, made in the image of the Lord, so that, left to itself, it could discern clearly and naturally the truths of the spiritual order. Such a faith, it will be seen, was in close harmony with the life of a dominantly agrarian nation, having a rather loose form of government, boasting of universal suffrage and safeguarding the rights of the common man.

Emerson, moreover, in his own Yankee manner, could grow intoxicated over the spirit of Reason; like the other Transcendentalists, he proceeded by a curious rationalizing to a belief in the justice and order of Nature which was constantly fortified by the new knowledge and the new science, so that he foresaw man, clairvoyant, free, living among the Emanations of the Universal Mind—the *noumena,* of course, of Immanuel Kant.

'We will walk on our own feet; we will work with our own hands; we will speak our own minds,' Emerson announced. 'A nation of men will for the first time exist, because each believes himself inspired by the Divine Soul. . . .' At the heart of the whole affair lay the native optimism, the positivism to which the author of Representative Men successfully appealed. 'The destiny of organized nature is amelioration, and who can tell its limits? . . . Great men exist that there may be greater men. . . . It is for man to tame the chaos; on every side whilst he lives, to scatter the seeds of science and song, that climate, corn, animals, men, may be milder, and the germs of love and benefit may be multiplied.'

Concord was deeply humanistic; surely by contrast with the age of the implacable Cotton Mather. It turned from the contemplation of God to that of the human race, by the adroit step of holding the human race God-like. It cultivated individualism even to great lengths of personal oddity, as in the case of Bronson Alcott and Thoreau. And one of its most amiable traits may have been the love of Nature, in the Concord meadows, under the great elms, by the mild river. Communing here with the eternal, the unvarying growths and the seasons, a mood of serenity and of dispelled passion was induced which was profoundly typical of the local spirit. It loved also learning, and with a vague 'uplift' air, the arts. One is convinced, at any rate, that never before in America had men's minds ranged so far in their readings, in their curiosities, in their speculations over the human *mores*, as they did on this historic soil, once famous as landmark of the rebellion against monarchy, now celebrated for its congregation of Yankee philosophers.

That which we call civilization is a frail and tenderly nourished organism, which can yet become hardily persistent once lodged in the prepared ground. Slow-growing, it is intricately composed of layer upon layer of the past and weathered into the particular, many-colored forms of the present. In New England we may glimpse the whole process of civilization, of culture, in miniature but clear example. Ideas played their part in the life of the country: between Beacon Hill in Boston and Emerson's Concord a certain dignity and vividness of character are evolved.

Concord was simply the flower of many generations of New England life. A common stock, patiently reared for two centuries, developing its local manners and legends, its local genius, within a given region, even the inhospitable soil that spread around Massachusetts Bay; a hierarchy creating order—it might be of priests and the wiser husbandmen, then of priests and merchants—these, at any rate, include the more necessary materials and conditions. So that after two hundred years, a homogeneous vision of the world, a native, racy expression of this, is arrived at and set in motion. At the prime, New England, through Concord, 'glowed with pure light.' A bloom, an inner grace, touched the thoughts and the intercourse of men during the heroic age of 'plain living and high thinking.'

Down to 1850 and even later, Henry Adams tells us, New England society, with a stability rare in American history, was directed by the professions. 'In politics, it was the old Ciceronian idea of government by the *best*' that produced the long line of New England statesmen. There was the rule of 'talent and wealth'; there were constants: there was always a succession of Adamses and their like who could be counted on, whose work could be judged according to values that had long existed in this world.

The philosophers of Concord watched over State Street sternly: they were aware of it almost as their *alter ego!* And in turn, the *haute-bourgeoisie*, directed by the Quincys, Everetts, Sumners, as well as the literary Boston of Ticknor, Prescott and Motley, were all equally aware of Concord. Indeed, out of its ferment of ideas there would be notions that repelled them; but there were others that they could take up and carry logically through the abyss of civil war.

The eager minds of the Yankee philosophers and poets often turned upon the society about them and examined its habits and its motives. Their indignation would grow vehement.

'The mass of men lead lives of quiet desperation,' said Thoreau from the retirement of his frog pond. They were occupied, even in this comparatively free country, only with the factitious cares and the superfluously coarse labors of life. They had no leisure for integrity, for manly relations with men. A man had no time to be 'anything but a machine.'

And Emerson, impatient of 'all the inequalities around us,' strenuously induced his Irish maid-servants to eat at the family table—although fear and hysteria had made the little domestic experiment abortive. Infected by his young friend Thoreau's enthusiasm, he had also tried to live off the soil himself, to graft apple-trees, to raise potatoes in the garden.

Emerson had known terrible misgivings about the world of his time. He resumed his doubts in his journal: 'I have the habitual feeling that the whole of our social structure—State, School, Religion, Marriage, Trade, Science—has been cut off from its roots in the soul. It would please me . . . to accept no church, state, school or society which did not found itself in my own nature. I should like to . . . abolish for myself all goods which are not a part of this good: to stand in the world *the fool of ideas* . . .

to renounce a property which is an accident to me.' The dissent of his friends at times took revolutionary form. There was the experiment of Brook Farm, a Fourierist or communal settlement, whose aim was to escape from the world of trade, to have men and women live together, work together at common tasks. in a coöperative phalanstery, 'so that leisure might be achieved to live in all the faculties of the human soul, leisure for art, books, and everything that ennobles.'

Emerson commented bravely: 'I approve every wild action of the experimenters. I say what they say . . .'

Margaret Fuller, one of the foremost of a line of mighty New England women, now founded *The Dial.* It was a natural outgrowth of the Concord ebullition; it was designed to mirror the ideas of the Transcendentalists, to be the organ of a native culture already 'mewing its mighty youth.' Emerson devised its program: 'He who doubts whether this age or this country can yield any contribution to the literature of the world only betrays his own blindness. Has the power of poetry ceased, or the need? Have the eyes ceased to see that which they would have? The heart beats in this age as of old and the passions are as busy as ever.' And in his voluminous journal where Emerson confides his intimate convictions and searchings he soliloquizes concerning *The*

Dial: 'I would not have it too purely literary. I wish we might make it a journal so broad and great in the survey that it should lead the opinion of this generation on every great interest, and read the law on property, government, education, as well as art, letters, religion. It does not seem worth our while to work with any other than sovereign aims. So I wish we might court some of the good fanatics and publish chapters on every head of the whole art of living.' And in effect, the poems and essays of Thoreau and Emerson, the 'Orphic Sayings' of Alcott, the writings of the radical divines, Parker and Ripley, all combined in an odd medley to appeal for freedom of ideas, to voice an ingenuous romantic faith in science, in unabated human progress such as passes all belief.

The environs of Boston, at any rate, were celebrated during the mid-century for their cultivation of the humanities. Ralph Waldo Emerson was veritably a local success. His metaphors and aphorisms entered the colloquial speech. His impressive appearance, his beautiful voice, fascinated a discriminating public. Even prosperous India merchants, these days, went wandering about the country with their umbrellas and their diaries in which to jot 'impressions of Nature.' The rage of Boston turned from parties to lectures. 'What with Waldo Emerson and Lowell Institute,' a contemporary witness notes, 'the whole world is squeezed through the pipe of science. All go to be filled, as the students of old went with their bowl for milk.' Dickens appeared and basked in a popularity such as no creature of the stage had yet won. Hawthorne's novels were accorded immortality. Great historians such as Prescott and Motley issued monumental works. Fanny Ellsler came to dance at the Boston Museum.

A grave argument relating to the famous *artiste*, appearing at this time in the pages of *The Dial*, is suggestive of the intellectual liberties which New England now permitted itself. The writer urged that it was morally permissible (despite her personal errors) to view the ballet dancer; and in obedience to this moral right and aesthetic duty, Emerson and Margaret Fuller went together to the concert. Neither of them had ever seen a ballet before, or knew what to expect. The dance began; both sat serenely silent. At last Emerson spoke:

'Margaret,' he said, 'this is poetry.'

'No, Waldo,' she replied, 'it is not poetry. It is religion.'

But interest now spread prodigiously to music and even to painting whose blessings were disseminated by their partisans with a quite missionary fervor.

'Give 'em a rousing discourse,' wrote James Russell Lowell to Story, the sculptor and poet, who had recently returned from Rome. 'Give a distant panoramic view of the lake of fire and brimstone that is prepared for all nations who don't love art, or who don't love it rightly!'

The New England thinkers advocated the arts with a fine moral fervor. Yet on the whole it was natural and just that their delights, their chief preoccupations, should be moral ones. The country needed moral leadership; and these men were responding to such a need with an earnestness that is rare in American annals. The pioneer spirit was far more brutal than we have been led to believe; the passions and mob movements of the Jacksonian era recently had been a caution to live through. At least Concord and circumambient New England exhibited all the vital character of a complete, ripening cultural organism. One hoped that by irradiation the power of this organism would spread beyond its own soil to embrace, to conquer the whole country.

2

What blight then fell upon them? What drouth withered their fruit?

We feel that the Transcendentalists had such a strong moral conscience as could play directly upon every phase of those social disasters that loomed already in the 1850's, that approached resistlessly. Was it strong enough to stand in a torrent, to escape being swept aside by great social cataclysms?

In the crises of the previous century Voltaire and

Rousseau had provided the conscience of Europe. The American, Dr. Paul Elmer More, commenting on the triumphant force of the author of *The Social Contract*, maintains that it was at bottom his *demoniac* personality, his inexplicable power, that imposed his ideas upon the world. Here there was no such single-minded ferocity. There was dissent from the ways of living of other men, but no program offered in their place. The New England conscience became, instead, something ethereal and remote, wrapping itself in its cloud-canopy of idealism and serenity; and in the crisis that approached for Americans, its part seems pitiable and bitterly insufficient.

Carlyle, the life-long friend of Emerson, scolded the New England idealists for their too great remove from the actual world. He urged that they return to 'their own poor nineteenth century, its follies and maladies, its blind or half-blind, but gigantic toilings, its laughter and its tears . . .' He wished also that some 'full-bodied Yankee man,' might emerge from among them, less the angel than the man.

The pilgrimage of the Yankee spirit, however, toward individual liberties and human graces, toward a freedom of ideas, led often to a certain *infantilism!* Something of the child-character, of the atmosphere of the Rollo books, clings to their generation. And it has not been remarked sufficiently that the ruling mind of the 'American Weimar' turned senile at a very early stage. While still almost in middle age,

Waldo Emerson could no longer remember faces and names . . .

He continued to soar, nevertheless. Fascinated by his own rhetoric it is as if he addressed with sightless eyes a host of presences in the void: 'I long for the hour when that supreme Beauty which ravished the souls of those Eastern men . . . shall speak to the West also—' etc. Was there in Emerson a growth and resourcefulness equal to the drastic changes of the time? Or was he only a merchant of the herbs and simples of wisdom, 'of the laws of Buddha and Plato mixed with a little Boston water,' as Mr. Van Wyck Brooks has declared? Thirty years after, even Whitman would note that Mr. Emerson keeps drawing on 'the same good pot of tea.'

In retrospect the curious contradictions of Yankee character even in its most serene form become more prominent and irritating. The shrewd mingled with the saintly and the childlike. One was transcendental in faith and practiced 'self-reliance' in life. One approved 'every wild action of the experimenters,' one pitied the poor—and yet held on to bank-stocks, as Emerson confessed in his journal. '*Don't run amuck against the world!*' is another notation in the valuable journal. The communism of Brook Farm was an extreme phase, but it must be remembered that Emerson treated the American Fourierists with a certain diffidence, while Hawthorne mocked at them. For that matter all the changes in the marriage institution that Fourier advocated were demurely avoided by the rebels of Concord: not the slightest breath of scandal was ever attached to the interesting community.

We conclude that the Transcendentalists believed fondly in the imminence of a transformation in human affairs which was somehow to be enacted *without gross visibility or violence.* For the personal freedom they required, the individualism they were prone to extol, they counted firmly on the persistence of 'decentralization' and the loose forms and institutions of democracy as Jefferson had conceived it. It was their doom, however, that a new order, a new centralization, a new absolutism beyond the dreams of the monstrous Hamilton, and all inimical to their reveries, was seizing rapidly on the country.

The ideas of Concord made little real headway beyond the line of the Hudson River; and in the end, by the great shiftings of the nation's axis, New England also lost her dominant position in trade.

When Emerson traveled in the west he saw America 'growing furiously, town and state; new Kansas, new Nebraska looming in these days, vicious politicians seething a wretched destiny for them already in Washington.' Wonder and stupefaction governed him. The farmers were only concerned with sections and quarter-sections of swamp land. 'There are no singing birds in the prairie, I truly heard,' he writes to Carlyle. All the life of the land and water had distilled no thought. 'Younger and better, I had no doubt been tempted to read and speak their sense for them. Now, I only gazed at them and their boundless land.'

He perceived, then, that it was vain and childlike to offer rewards of a moral nature to this race.

3

The more one reflects on the frequent emergence, during the earlier American period, of strongly demarcated, highly individual artistic character—such as the gracefully ironic, melancholy Hawthorne, the aesthetic, infinitely inventive Edgar Poe, the exotic Herman Melville, the epic Whitman—the more one leans to the notion that the libertarian atmosphere of the republic, in its youth, tolerated and encouraged such individualism. For outside of New England, in benighted, frivolous New York of the 'Knickerbocker' era, three extraordinary men appeared: Poe, Whitman, and Melville.

Even if only on the fringes of the provincial society, an Edgar Poe might flourish a little, fascinating literary females by his fertile genius, his sad excesses. In the absence of traditions or criteria in pleasure-loving New York, his romantic poses and mannerisms and his air almost of a mountebank could win attention to verses that soon became proverbial. It is true as well that the absence of all models and traditions, such as that, for instance, of bohemianism, or a moderated libertinism, worked adversely for him, since nothing guided or stayed him from pure self-destruction.

And yet far from thinking Poe a 'chemical monster,' an anomaly existing on a plane outside of his time, tormented by enemies and poverty, I feel rather that Poe had his little day, that the age encouraged such prodigiousness as his, that poverty weighed little on him, certainly less than heredity.

His career had been one of sheer demonstration of genius, rather than of accomplishment. One conceives his nature as a dominantly inventive, creative one, rushing in versatile fashion from one type of activity to another, taking no time to stake his claims, while throwing off suggestions, discoveries without end, for artistic posterity to explore.

Resisting the 'Didactic' and the voice of moral duty which sounded so irritatingly for him from Boston, he professed to make beauty solely the province of the poem. He spoke of the poem *per se,* of writing the 'poem simply for the poem's sake.' And he shocked his time by exposing the deliberate artifice with which *The Raven* had been composed, step by step, 'with the precision and the rigid consequence of a mathematical problem.'

He had carried literature out of the English romantic revolution with which he came, toward an abstract perfection, toward an intellectual finality. The love of artifice, of form, of related suggestions and symbolisms, was a cerebral passion with him. The celebrated lines of *The City in the Sea,*

> . . . whose wreathed friezes intertwine
> The viol, the violet, and the vine,

were to haunt generations. Their art, suggesting virtually a refuge from life, an end in itself, was to be carried to Europe by the sympathy of a Baudelaire before it returned to America again.

He elevated Taste above the Moral Sense, as he said; but Intellect, or rather, intellectual curiosity, ruled him above all. In early youth he had written a *Sonnet to Science;* none loved truth, he asserted, more than he. His intellectualism was lavished upon the intricate mystery tales which are like mathematical problems and upon mathematical problems which are poems. Toward the end he ventured in *Eureka,* half earnest, half trivial, speculations which sound to us now like the most daring auguries of modern science! He suggests strongly the 'experimental man' of universal mind, one whom Paul Valéry has likened to Leonardo.

Beyond the intellectual curiosity and zest that was so natural to this American generation, there were contrasting qualities in Poe's art, such as the obsession with the supernatural. What caused this? Was it an escape from a surrounding ugliness which one did not even comment on in the stress of greater preoccupations and under the sense of a fated detachment? At any rate the supernatural was a strain which was to be handed down, and which would stamp and characterize nearly all the later literature.

4

The American of today who lives in an utterly 'centralized' world, who trembles for his life at each street corner, who heeds the admonition of traffic lights or the growled order to 'step lively!'—the American who travels in thronged trains, who labors within a human chain, who snatches in terror his forbidden liquor; the American who accepts his opinions and his information from the radio-receiver, the cinema, the bill-poster, the press—this American is utterly unfit to understand the degree of human liberty which was enjoyed in the United States up to the days of the Civil War.

The Presidents during this equalitarian epoch hitched their horses to a tethering-post with their own hands before mounting the steps of the capitol. *On trébuchait sur des vaches*, the French ambassador wrote home: one literally bumped into cows on the steps of the capitol. Yet one need only recall the splendid equipages of Washington, great landed noble that he was, to perceive how deliberately the negligences of a Jefferson and a Jackson departed from previous forms, and how the spirit of the Jacobins had swept over the country in the early part of the century. Both leaders had represented the triumph of the agrarian party over the Federalist merchants and bankers.

'I dread the day when the people are piled one upon another in the cities!' Jefferson had exclaimed. And his followers had labored to keep America dominantly a nation of tillers of the soil and to hold in check the faction of capitalism to whom they were naturally opposed. The farmer and the free artisan looked with joy at a government which governed as little as possible, which left the country decentralized, which had accorded them those universal rights of the vote withheld largely in the first days of the confederation. The future was large, the bounties of nature in their land vast, and they believed confidently that the riches which belonged to the people would be distributed generously and equally to the people and never again to hereditary barons or favorites of the despot. There were evils and excesses, to be sure, which irked—but an American was his own master; in this large free country he could always move on to free soil, live off the fat, black, loamy earth of the west and yield obeisance to none.

The shifting, fluid character of a frontier society could be unbeautiful enough; the absence of all program, the purely negative liberties and laxities of the time would permit the enemy of the free farmer and the free artisan to entrench himself and ultimately to seize control of the government; but for all that, the spectacle of human freedom in the aggregate, so comparatively new and rare in the world, still intoxicated early American thinkers with pride. Faith in the common man, faith in the goodness, the *divinity*, of the natural, untrammeled human being who bowed to no superior, was passionately preached, as we have seen, in Concord. It gained an even more excessive and impassioned spokesman in Walt Whitman.

One visualizes with amazement the carefree youth of Whitman in the 1830s. He could leave his work, carpentry or journalism, and go swimming for the afternoon in the beautiful surf of Long Island. He would go running naked along the shore, as he related, shouting the lines of Homer—was it Chapman's translation?—into the wind and the booming sea. He haunted the ferries of the East River, scanned the bracing harbor with its numberless sails, frequented cab-drivers, laborers, policemen, Broadway, the beer cellar of Pfaff's, where journalists and literati gathered. He wore a high hat and a boutonnière. 'Throughout this period,' his friend John Burroughs relates, 'it is enough to say that he sounded all experiences of life, with all their passions, pleasures and abandonments. He was young, in perfect bodily condition, and had the city of New York and its ample opportunities around him. . . .'

And then, after much free wandering down roads from Canada to New Orleans, from New York almost to the Rockies, a great change came over him. He read the message of Emerson and absorbed the humanism of Concord: 'Let me admonish you, first of all, to go alone, to refuse the good models, even those which are sacred in the imaginations of men. . . . "I also am a man." . . . Yourself a new-born bard, cast behind you all conformity, and acquaint man at first hand with the Deity.'

Whitman abandoned his high hat, his flower; he assumed simple clothes, the collar open at the neck. He became a *sansculotte;* he spoke from soap-boxes for Free Trade, Free Labor, Free Soil. He abandoned journalism for carpentry, while he tranquilly planned his book.

After continued ambitions and efforts, as he said, to take part in the 'great mêlée' for the usual rewards, he now found himself possessed by one special conviction and purpose. It was 'to articulate and faithfully express in literary or poetic form, and uncompromisingly, my own physical, emotional, moral, intellectual and aesthetic Personality, in the midst of, and tallying the momentous spirit and facts . . . of current America.' This heroic and epic purpose was also to be executed 'in a far more candid and comprehensive sense than any hitherto poem or book.'

There is no questioning the logic and the resolution of *Leaves of Grass.* Whitman meditated his book for four years. It was to be a song to the free individual, the free ego, and through him a song of the liberated humanity whom he represented. It was to be the literature of equality and 'progress' implicit in American life for half a century. He was to be, in short, the bard of democracy.

He began with Walt Whitman, the body of Walt Whitman, nay the toenails of Walt Whitman, and moved on to the Soul—placing all of this against the panorama of American movement and life. His verses were written with that metrical and rhythmic lawlessness that was in the air of the time, examples of which are to be found in the rhapsodic fragments of Thoreau and Emerson. And as he viewed himself in relation to the age, he resolved that the high function of the national bard, which he desired to be, was a kind of leadership through prophecy. His book was to be apocalyptic, with auguries of perfection through science, of comradeship, of ennobled maternity, of athleticism, of peace, and an era of learning and art to be attained by the children of democracy. His intense patriotism, amounting almost to aggression, must not be likened to that of bankers who finance wars and hunt down dissenters; it was the primitive nationalism which based itself on his pride in the free institutions of America during the youth of the republic.

Whitman, carried away by his vision, by the rôle

of demiurge which he saw for himself, printed his own book, and unhesitatingly wrote his own reviews:

'*An American Bard at last!*—We shall cease shamming and be what we really are! We shall start an athletic and defiant literature! . . .'

He addressed crowds, lectured, sold copies of *Leaves of Grass* himself. One can only liken him to William Blake, who celebrated the French Revolution by donning a red cap and rushing about the streets of London all alone.

Emerson saluted him, naturally and bravely—but an outcry of disgust greeted the circulation of the strange work. The physiological catalogue of the 'body electric' in its unabashed paganism evoked horror in high and low places: 'Impious libidinousness—the exulting audacity of Priapus-worshiping obscenity,' was the typical dictum. A motley group of ill-matched admirers came to Whitman's defense, to be sure. He was following with the mingled emotions of his ingenuous and candid egoism the slow, almost imperceptible, progress of his book on the now turbulent ocean of American life, when the Civil War came upon them with such a fury of iron and blood in which worlds founder.

5

The laxities, the 'decentralized' character, of the pre-war era tolerated the populism of Channing,

Emerson, and Whitman, the 'anarchism' of Thoreau, and the aestheticism of Poe. And likewise, favored by the same libertarian atmosphere, the personality of Herman Melville could develop itself freely during the innocent '40s and '50s of New York. His particular dissent, his presentiments and skepticisms, could persist for a time within the loose folds of a society which imposed as yet no great common regimentation upon all minds. But when all the loose threads of the social body are drawn tightly in, when all is knit firmly together in great collectivities, horde movements—then the dissenting individual finds himself *déclassé* to an unheard-of degree. His situation becomes untenable, his opposition sinister; it is as if the fingers of all men pointed accusingly at him.

The case of Herman Melville thus appears one of the most tragic of all in that earlier era. The whole drama of the situation—the drama that is typical of the later and darker age—plays fully upon him as his life prolongs itself amid the desolate changes of the post-bellum times. It has been said of his contemporaries Emerson and Whitman that they had no sense of evil; and Poe after all was dead. Melville experienced the great alterations of the whole surface of life in America as a personal disaster. After the short flight of glory he knew only isolation and such *indifference* as few men of genius have ever borne. He felt himself defeated by his milieu; he became silent and abandoned his art.

Herman Melville's passion for individual liberty was even more imperative than that of the Concord men. Voyaging before the mast, whaling for years in the Pacific, he made of the oceans his Walden Pond. All the movements of his youth seem infatuated and impulsive. 'Sad disappointments . . . united with a naturally roving disposition,' he tells us, directed him to 'the watery world.' And so, habitually, his books open with a ship slipping her cables and fleeing musically from the land. For earth is fatal to the ship; and it is apparent that 'all deep earnest thinking is but the intrepid effort of the soul to keep to the open independence of her sea, while the wildest winds of heaven and earth conspire to cast her on the treacherous, slavish shore.'

Melville's dreams are overpowering. Far out from the land, swaying from the mainmast over tropical seas, he abandons himself to his reveries and he is at peace with himself.

When Melville returned from the South Seas after four years of prodigious adventuring on the ocean and among savages, he could not be silent about what he had seen and experienced. *Typee* and *Omoo*, written in 1845, are the ingenuous, ungarnished narratives of his wanderings in the Orient and his life among the Marquesan Islanders.

Melville's defense of the pagans strikes one as something highly original in its time. Yet the picture of an earthly Paradise, of the happy nakedness and natural beauty of his savages, aroused only mistrust among the little tradespeople who formed his public. He is read as a matter of scandal, attains a cheap celebrity as one who has lived among cannibals, while the press attacks him for his 'cool, sneering wit,' for his 'voluptuous pictures . . . his loathful lechery.'

His attitude is in reality similar to that of the cult in France which adored the 'Hurons' before the Revolution, as is evinced by his outbursts against missionaries and the 'vices and enormities of a tainted civilization.'

Living on tropical fruits, swimming with the young 'river-nymphs,' joying in their games, amused, mystified, or regaled by their strange dances and rituals, this young and early neophyte of Rousseau and eighteenth century Naturism—this enemy of nineteenth century progress had learned to mistrust the culture of white men. There are spirited passages in Melville which curiously match the 'anarchism' of Thoreau.

'There were none of those thousand sources of irritation,' Herman Melville writes, 'that the ingenuity of civilized man has created to mar his own felicity. There were no foreclosures of mortgages, no protested notes, no debts of honor in Typee; no unreasonable tailors . . . no assault and battery attorneys to foment discord, backing their clients up to a quarrel and then knocking their heads together; no destitute widows starving on the cold charities of the world; no debtors' prison, no proud and hard-hearted Nabobs: or to sum up all in one word—no Money!'

Nor were there withered spinsters, nor lovesick maidens, nor melancholy young men. All was mirth, fun, and high good humor. The wonder is that Melville ever desired to escape from these aborigines, who were, for him, masters of the art of living.

Once youth had passed, once the gay Triton was moored to the deceptive land, anchored to family and all the charges of a scribbler's toilsome life, systematic misfortune, a Nemesis—the unhappy fatality of the American artist, as Henry James imagined it—pursued Melville. It is as if his heedless youth, which had been too happy, *belonged to another century*. 'Dollars damn me,' he writes to Hawthorne; 'what I feel most moved to write, that is banned. . . . I am so pulled hither and thither by circumstances. The calm, the coolness, the silent, grass-growing mood, in which a man ought to compose—that I fear can seldom be mine.'

His inherited temperament was difficult and complex: he may even have been perverse, and his domestic existence, therefore, deeply troubled beneath the surface. Above all a sense of desperate alienation from the life about him weighed upon him. Thus the huge, rambling epic of *Moby-Dick*, written in a gloomy back room of New York during the sweltering summer of 1851, is a book of anger. Originating as a compendium on the whale fishery, *Moby-Dick* formed itself as a narrative of Promethean struggle, a great Odyssey across the globe in chase of the symbolic 'white whale,' which, touching wildly all the notes of great literature, clings always to an interior plan, a marching order.

'Call me Ishmael!' he cries, and he is off with a boatload of ruffians for that watery world in whose 'landlessness alone resides the highest truth, shoreless, indefinite as God—'

Baffled or resigned, melancholy or irresponsible, Melville suggests from now on one of those solitary and 'dangerous' characters of literary history, Blake, Poe, Baudelaire, Rimbaud. Entering the house of Melville and examining the evidence still to be seen—all the smashed and broken objects—we have inevitably the sense of a lonely struggle that has taken place within these walls, one that led logically to a kind of abjuration of everything.

Melville was aware that for a public success he must write 'the *other* way,' express somehow the complacency of the prosperous time. He had growing within him the sense of opposing the hosts of 'commonness and conventionalism and worldly prudent-mindedness.' And in *Pierre: or the Ambiguities*, he had written—with less felicity, but with no resort to allegory—a problem novel whose theme may be likened to Shelley's *The Cenci,* attacking existing institutions and offering the case of a moral conscience in arms against the proprieties of the Philistines. Preceding so early the trend of the later realistic social novels, the book begot a brutal reception which effectually ended the career of the author.

Pierre is himself imagined in revolt against society. The author broods upon those 'subterranean rivers flowing through the caverns of man,' and on 'the relentless law of earthly fleetingness.' He is convinced by now of 'the mere imaginariness of the supposed solidest principles of human associations.' He sees that 'all the world does never gregariously advance to truth, but only here and there some of its individuals do; and by advancing leave the rest behind; cutting themselves further adrift from their sympathies . . . and making themselves regarded with downright fear and hate. What wonder then that those advanced minds should often be goaded into turning round in acts of wanton aggression upon sentiments and opinions now forever left in their rear.'

And now Melville (always assuming *Pierre* to be intrinsically confession) imagines himself Hamlet; or now Dante, exiled, and having received 'unforgivable affronts' from the world, bequeathing 'his immortal curse to it.' He rises again to the Promethean apostrophe of *Moby-Dick:*

'Ye Heavens . . . I call to ye! If to follow Virtue

to her uttermost vista, where common souls never go; if by that I take hold on Hell, and the uttermost virtue after all proves but a betraying pander to the monstrousest vice—then close in and crush me, ye stony walls, and into one gulf let all things tumble together.'

But actually Melville recoiled from the gesture of revolt—and we touch here the veritable problem of his soul, a paralyzing introspection—as he reveals in *Pierre* his own temporizings, falterings, regrets. He knows how 'the never entirely repulsed hosts of Commonness and Conventionalism return to the charge, press hard upon the faltering soul, and with inhuman hootings deride all its nobleness. The man is as seized by the arms and legs and convulsively pulled either way by his own indecisions and doubts. . . . All round and round does the world lie, as in a sharpshooter ambush to pick off the beautiful illusions of youth by the pitiless cracking rifles of the realities of the age.'

Melville's revolt is thus deflected. It takes a curious midway course between that of two other 'rebels' close to his time: Poe and Whitman. Poe moved fatally toward his self-destruction; and Whitman, with his unclouded and simple animality, detaches himself serenely from the Philistines and wanders down his open road. In Melville all resistance subsides abruptly, as far as one can see. He schools himself to silence, to playing out tonelessly a sedate existence. But this is a mask. . . .

In 1856 Herman Melville, in ill health, made one of his last voyages, a tour as far as the Holy Land. 'All spirit of adventure is now gone from me,' he told Hawthorne in England. At this sad period he fell to writing poems, as a consolation, and we know that this was deemed an ominous sign of distraction by his family.

Clarel, the long poem, that was only to be published privately many years later, illuminates the silent period of nearly forty years. One reads the reflections of his defeat:

> My kin—I blame them not at heart—
> Would have me act some routine part,
> Subserving family, and dreams
> Alien to me—

In his distress, he cries like Baudelaire, 'This world clean fails me!' It concerns him, then, to find some 'other world'—but where? 'In creed?' Alas! faith, as Hawthorne said, was wanting in him.

He felt himself an enemy of the rising industrial age, the new democratic America of 'mines and marts'; and this is extremely significant. He bursts into imprecations: 'democracy is the . . . harlot on horseback . . . the great Diana of ill-fame, the arch-strumpet.'

Melville longed for freedom, for liberty of conscience—surely as much as Emerson or Whitman ever did; but with a clairvoyance that neither possessed, he foresaw democracy, under mechanism, preparing its own degraded level. In a vein of prophecy he foretells how the modern society makes way for 'the new Hun,' how the masses were to become 'coolies' again:

> Relapse barbaric may impend,
> Dismissal into ages blind—moral dispersion.

None listened to his warnings; none heard them, to be sure. In a short time Melville had abandoned the pen, the very act of writing having become futile and repugnant to him:

> Why then?
> Remaineth to me what? The pen?
> Dead factor of ethereal life!

Certainly he recoiled before the task of imposing his views upon a hostile age. He would progress always toward a more intense inward contemplation, casting off all exterior 'vanities.' He is banished, but with his mystic belief of a Schopenhauer in man's destiny of suffering he has found escape, obscurely, silently, along the road to nirvana: 'I pray for peace —for nothingness—for the feeling of myself, as of some plant, absorbing life, without seeking it, and existing without sensation. I feel that there can be no perfect peace in individualness. Therefore I hope one day to feel myself drunk up into the pervading spirit animating all things. . . .'

Herman Melville, a gentleman of patrician Dutch and New England stock, played a strange part in the clamorous bustling American world of the later nineteenth century. He became an outdoor custom-house clerk in New York and for two decades took the same steps between office and home. Nearly two generations would pass him by; the pullulating life of America would roll noisily on, elbowing the forgotten man in the streets of Manhattan.

6

One may trace the currents of unrest in all their vibrations, through every walk of life, even to the second or third generation, and the lesson remains identical: humanistic and libertarian impulses radiated from New England, and chiefly from Concord, but enjoyed only a short-lived career, being soon cut down by the material power of the factory dynasty which raised itself in the very heart of New England.

The enlightenment of Concord had extended its authority and won friends throughout the country; it was as if ideas, for a time, raced vainly with the powerful economic tide that had been set in motion.

In New York, during the generation preceding the Civil War, one of the most elegant and cultivated personalities was surely the elder Henry James, whose curious philosophical researches and writings have been shadowed by the luster of his two sons. He was a man whose example formed quite a monstrous exception to that of his contemporaries. The son of a great Albany merchant, he had studied for the ministry, but had abandoned this career in one of those spiritual crises so characteristic of the times. Under the inspiration of Swedenborg he had resolved to devote himself to seeking 'the true relation between mankind and its creator' and had affirmed his unconventional and original points of view in one book after another. He had become a friend of Emerson by natural sympathy and had long been in intimate rapport with the philosophers of Concord and of *The Dial.*

Rich by inheritance, he managed his great fortune passively; for he was as indifferent to trade as he was aggressive in pursuit of ideas. He had come to New York after his marriage, and his growing and, indeed, remarkable family had found an anchorage for some ten years in a great house on Fourteenth Street.

Perhaps almost alone in New York, Henry James, Sr., desired to live the good life, in the richest possible sense. For he had been to Europe to widen his horizons; he had talked for long hours with the great Carlyle, he had heard Michelet and devoured the books of Renan; he had saturated himself in the great galleries of Paris where the 'golden riot' of civilization was visible. And now he caused pictures and prints to come from Europe; the great Victorian novels were read aloud in his home, along with the exciting and authoritative *Revue des Deux Mondes* and *Punch*. And he entertained lavishly: the friendly fireside of Fourteenth Street was haunted by artists and authors, by the celebrities of England and Europe, and even by famous actors. Among early New Yorkers, Bryant and Irving were to be seen at the James home, and Edgar Poe, 'our ill-starred magician, whose rhymes were hummed everywhere,' as the younger Henry James relates. Perhaps the New England group of George Ripley, Theodore Parker, Dana, and Curtis were most in view here; and above all Emerson, who would pause gratefully in his travels at the home of his old friend, and for whom there was 'Mr. Emerson's room.'

'I visualize,' one of the sons recalls vividly, 'the winter firelight of our back-parlor at dusk, and the great Emerson—I knew he was great, greater than any of our friends—sitting in its glow between my parents, before the lamps had been lighted. . . . Elegantly slim, benevolently aquiline, and commanding a tone alien, beautifully alien to any we heard roundabout . . . as he bent his benignity on me by an invitation to draw nearer to him, off the hearth-rug . . . I knew myself in touch with the wonder of Boston. The wonder of Boston was above all, just then and there for me, in the sweetness of the voice and the finish of the speech. Was this not my first glimmer of a sense that the human tone *could*, in that independent and original way, be interesting?'

One lingers over this remarkable bourgeois *foyer* of an extinguished New York, as much for the bright and courageous effort of the father as for the episode of genius in bud, in the shape of William and Henry James, amid so much conversation and suggestion, in an atmosphere virtually of an American 'revival of learning.'

The education of the five James children—for there were the still younger Wilkie and Robertson and Alice—was unconventional in the deepest sense. They were much tutored in this fortunate family. The father followed their education closely and yet with a curious skepticism; for, conscious of the revolutions taking place then in science and faith, he was splendidly impatient of formality, of the merely academic, of traditional schooling.

In a world that bristled with trade, he conducted himself as if he were utterly bent on preserving his children from such actualities. He groped for a certain freedom in their education, urging always, in his many walks with William and Henry, the interests of character and conduct. Pedantries were his anathema on this ground, and he would make hay of moralisms and offer so many odd declarations that 'there was the presence of paradox bright among us.' And when Henry James recollects vaguely, long afterward, how his father's chief concern was for their 'spiritual decency,' holding that this was profession and career enough; how instead of making their education 'pay,' his design was 'to make life interesting' for them—one senses almost the pathos of the Transcendentalist effort to fortify the spirit against the already darkly foreseen tendencies of the age. In the mood of the high optimistic transition which he floated in, Henry James, Sr., hoped pathetically that through one's spiritual force alone one might succeed in mitigating the harsher conditions.

There was already such a squalor and brou-ha-ha about New York. It was 'grim' New York, whose commerce roared and clattered along cobbled streets in carts and carriages. Along Fifth Avenue, the great rickety billboards blazed with the appeal of 'Mr. Barnum' and his revelations of bottled mermaids and bearded ladies. Yet on Eighteenth Street there was 'a country place, with grounds, animals, farm life.' Union Square was still inclosed by a high iron grill, but one preferred Washington Square with its quiet fountain and the fine trees and the dead leaves that stirred crisply under one's feet in autumn. And in near-by Waverly Place, 'the small red houses of the south side carried the imagination back already to a vanished order.'

The early life of the Jameses was lived virtually on a safety raft, 'floating upon too high a tide of the ugly and the graceless'—even of the violent and the sinister, one might add, if one recalled the relations of contemporaries like Herman Melville which picture the unpaved streets in darkness, the 'flashy' types along Broadway, the line of glittering taverns, the procession of street-walkers, footpads, the descents of brutal police. . . .

Floating, then, on this groaning and turbid torrent, the James home sounded its submerged note of culture. Amid the hawking and barter and ruse and violence, the elder Henry James offered his own admirable example, practiced his own kind of 'consistency, intensity, brilliancy.'

There were times when they suffered for their odd education. At the very proper school which Henry James, Jr., attended with so many little Phelpses, Stokeses, Havemeyers, Colgates, of later eminence, he would be asked what church they belonged to. And his father would reply: 'We don't go to any. But don't we belong to all of them? At any rate tell them that we're excluded from the communion of none!'

And above all his classmates seemed perplexed that the head of the family was not 'in business.' In deep embarrassment Henry James, Jr., besought his father for an explanation. 'Say I'm a philosopher, say I'm a seeker for truth, say I'm a lover of my kind, say I'm an author of books, if you like; or best of all, just say I'm a Student! . . .'

How long could the household, glowing with the transcendental enlightenment, sustain itself in New York?

In the end, after ten years, Henry James, Sr., had come to fear New York; he feared it for his sons. Its clamor and its trafficking grew daily louder as the city enlarged itself, spread its business district farther and farther 'uptown,' rebuilding itself and destroying all landmarks, while the merciless torrent of trade veritably tossed their little 'safety raft' higher and higher upon angry waves.

'Considering with much pity our four stout boys,' he wrote his friend Emerson, 'who have no playroom within doors and import shocking bad manners from the street, we gravely ponder whether it would not be better to go abroad for a few years with them, allowing them to absorb French and German, and get such a sensuous education as they cannot get here.'

And so he had uprooted his whole family, dismantled the great, jolly Fourteenth Street home in 1855, and carried them off to the old Calvinistic city of Geneva, by the lake, in view of Mont Blanc. For three or four years they were to be expatriated, while Henry James, Jr., at thirteen received his first sharp and wonderful impressions of a Europe which he would hunger for forever after. When they returned, it would be to haunt Newport, a little promontory of the disillusioned and the *raffinés*—Newport, with its opera-glass turned forever toward Europe, with its gossip of the grand tour.

New York but courted such disruptions and uprootings. In the great shifting scene, where with a ringing of hammer and nails a strenuous new order was being erected, every day the fragile effort of civilization became dismayed, and after a brief struggle to persist, turned sickly or fled; if one returned in a few years, all one's memories had been swept away in the name of utility. Henry James, Jr., was to return long after and contemplate with stupefaction the devastated scene of his birth and of his boyhood, blighted under skyscrapers or department stores.

'What would I have been? What would I have been,' he would wonder, 'if I had stayed?'

II

THE BELATED REVELERS

One generation abandons the enterprise of another like stranded vessels.—THOREAU.

EVER since one could remember, the Americans had been wrecking and building for their larger Manifest Destiny. They surveyed wild swamps and plotted the course of the roaring thoroughfares of tomorrow.

In 1840 the French observer, Alexis de Tocqueville, had visited the immense cleared site on the banks of the Potomac. In this muddy village, no larger than Pontoise, they were making place for a capital of a million souls! And with much prescience, though they made their public works vast enough, they did not plan them to endure long. One saw from a distance the white palaces, the pillared façades, and nearing, found them to be of painted wood. . . .

The hastily erected temples, now classical, now of genteel scroll-work or even Gothic, grew quickly old, without decency or loveliness, as all sensitive Americans could see. The progress of the new cities took the lines of the land speculator; utterly given over to the swift game of enterprise and growth, the new men joined the rush, the crusade toward immeasurable riches, toward physical prosperity. Everything about him seemed to unite in drawing the native of the United States earthward; and those who sought beauty, plastic or intellectual, must look elsewhere, almost to another world.

In the end they would discover 'that *progress cannot long be made in the application of the sciences without cultivating the theory of them;* that all the arts are perfected by one another; and that, however much they may be absorbed by the principal objects of their desires, *it is necessary to turn aside from it frequently, in order the better to attain it in the end.*'

It was Europe, with its 'centers of illumination,' with its tastes for the pleasures of the mind, that served as a great incubator of ideas which could be exploited on the frontier. The political theories, the discoveries of physicists and doctors, the fashions of literature and dress, had all been drawn from the mother continent. Even the modernity which we invariably associate with American life was in those days attached rather to Paris or London.

For a long time imaginative Americans turned to Europe both for 'inspiration' and for profit. The travelers of the great literary period are proverbial: Longfellow and Irving found atmosphere in Europe and sold it at home; Prescott and Motley became the historians of Spain and Holland. Their impulse is defined by the much-traveled Hawthorne, who, though longing to be 'intensely American,' lamented the difficulty of creating his romances about a country 'where there is no shadow, no antiquity, no mystery, no picturesque and gloomy wrong, nor anything but a broad and commonplace prosperity, in broad and simple daylight, which is happily the case with my dear native land.'

As they grew more conscious of their needs, however, and of a certain *malaise* experienced constantly in the native environment, American artists departed in greater and greater numbers for England, France, and Italy, and formed thus an important precedent which remained alive for many generations.

From a world that was changing an exodus of artists, sculptors, and poets had begun even during the sad years preceding the Civil War. They were a small host of artless seekers of knowledge, would-be haunters of the fountainhead; yet in sating their personal thirsts these itinerant Americans who aspired to philosophize, to build, to carve, played also a larger, impersonal part in extending the American consciousness to partake of the great currents of the world.

Europe held 'wonders' for them; it was the real *fontaine de jouvence;* and when they returned, glowing with their impressions, others now hung on their lips and sighingly acknowledged their loss.

'Art,' writes Henry James, in his study of William Wetmore Story, 'in the easy view of the age, was to be picked up in the favoring air—if the influence invoked was clearly, in their own air, invoked in vain, so, inevitably, the good people of that time thought of it as resident in the air that in all the world differed most from their own. There, presumably, it hung in clusters and could be eaten from the tree, so that to be free of the mystery one had but to set sail and partake.'

They started on their *Wanderjahre*, surely as none others had ever done, for the golden isles. They came to partake of the cloying-sweet, the rich feast of Italy, the grace of Florence, the thrill of Rome. They voyaged under primitive conditions, in the clipper ships, in the first side-wheelers. They wandered across Europe by ox-cart and traversed the Alps in carriages, amid war and barricade. Often they looked at all things from the standpoint of that little clod of western earth which they carried about with them as the good Mohammedan his strip of carpet on which he kneels down, facing toward Mecca. They might be revolted like the puritanical Hawthorne at the spectacle of 'undressed images'; or if New Englanders, in general, consumed by the long habit of hating England. Yet in other cases their personalities dissolved, were modified, even disintegrated, under the corrupting atmosphere. Some were lost to the White Devil of Italy; others succumbed to the facile Bohemianism of Paris.

The motive of the earlier poets, who were still so close to the romantic English movements, was invariably to idle and to invite the picturesque, as did Irving in the precincts of Granada.[1] There was a certain release enjoyed from the perceptible pressure of American life, which is well expressed by a young poet lounging about the Piazzo San Marco in 1860: 'Repose takes you to her inmost heart,' writes the youthful Howells in his *Venetian Days*, 'and you learn her secrets—arcana unintelligible to you in the new-world life of bustle and struggle.'

There were cases, to be sure, of more passionate rebellion which lured the errant American, at times, to strange paths and even tragic adventures. One of the most moving of these is the story of the brilliant Margaret Fuller, whose apparent sexual intensity and revolutionary ardor had driven her from the little world of Concord, with its atmosphere of 'a large, square high-windowed room, all clean and cool and bare of rubbish.' She had met Mazzini in New York and set forth for insurgent Italy in '48. In Rome she had delighted in the monuments and palaces of the past, while aiding the revolutionary cause of the

[1] It is now suspected that Washington Irving may have done a great deal of romantic philandering in Italy that was little consonant with his professed conservative, puritanical principles. Important documents, long concealed by cautious descendants, may do much to alter our notions of the great dead. Americans abroad, we grow convinced, *have always been the same;* but in former days they held their tongue about much that was learned in foreign lands. . . .

present. She had fallen in love with the Count Ossoli, a young insurrectionist, and she had nursed the wounded in the hospital and at the barricades. When the insurrection was put down she had had to flee with her lover and her child, only to perish all in shipwreck within sight of New York.

The lot of the painter was hard. Not only did the native world seem forbidding and bare to his brush, but there was an absolute want of the conditions favorable to a good apprenticeship: there were no teachers, there were no models, there were no objects of beauty, no galleries, virtually no contemporary awareness of the technique of art, no stimulating example and competition. The talented portrait painters of the late eighteenth century, such as West, had simply crossed the ocean and felt no incentive to return. The later generation of Washington Allston, William Page, William Wetmore Story, and George Inness had lived in Italy for long years and had fared badly on the whole.

The instance of Story, the sculptor and poet who was the son of the great Massachusetts justice, holds us longest, for the symptoms of intellectual unrest that it reveals—an unrest, instability, exoticism, that was to become the definite character of the succeeding generations.[2] Toward 1850, William Story had settled with his family in Rome, in the permanent

[2] It is highly significant that Henry James devoted himself, late in life, to a biography of Story and his friends, the circle of exiles-for-art whom he met in Rome.

Anglo-American colony. It was the period of Italomania, and besides the obscure Americans, persons like the Brownings, Walter Savage Landor, and other frequenters of the romantic or classical spirit played their part in this international microcosm.

One reads in the early letters how Story had gone to the Pitti Palace every day, how he had stood in a crowd to watch the Pope wash the feet of pilgrims, how he listened to the chorus of the Sistine Chapel, while gaping at the 'awful and mighty figures of Michael Angelo looking down from the ceiling'; how he had lingered in St. Peter's 'while the gloom of evening was gathering in the lofty aisles and shrouding the frescoed domes.'

The beautiful Italian years slipped by, and life in America seemed 'less and less satisfactory in retrospect,' as he wrote to his friends James Russell Lowell and Charles Sumner.

There had been curious casualties among the early artists. They taught themselves strangely. In the case of William Page, all the promise, the achieved talent, to which so many allusions are found, vanishes in a darkness which was the result of some fallacious theory as to pigments!

'*His fate,*' Henry James observed in his biography of Story, '*represents after all the clumsy waste, the unlighted freedom of experiment possible only in provincial conditions.* And his idea of himself all the while was that he was at school to Titian!'

And there was also Washington Allston, whose rare relics knew fame for a time in incongruous old parlors and over the old pianos, glooming out sadly above Victorian sofas. Allston was another victim of 'blighting conditions.' He was to end by painting less and less. After twenty years devoted to his one huge canvas, *Daniel Before Belshazzar*, it was unfinished, and the vaguely obliterating strokes of his decline had left only glimpsed fragments of the earlier charm.

When Story, who was his friend, returned for a visit to Boston in 1856, he at once ascribed Allston's misfortune to the hostile environment: 'Allston starved spiritually in Cambridgeport; he fed upon himself. There was nothing congenial without, and he turned all his powers inward and drained his memory dry. His works grew thinner and vaguer every day, and in his old age he ruined his great picture. I know no more melancholy sight than he was, so rich and beautiful a nature, in whose veins the south ran warm, which was born to have grown to such height, and to have spread abroad such fragrancy, stunted on the scant soil and withered by the cold winds of Cambridgeport. I look at his studio, whenever I pass, with a heart-pang. It's a terrible ghost—all is in fact ghostlike here. . . .'

Story himself had undergone little true discipline, little that constituted training. He had absorbed; he had fed himself with impressions so that he might produce. But he had completed almost nothing of value.

He was obsessed, however, by the lesson of Allston, and feared himself to become a victim of the lack of standards in such things. 'One must have an audience,' he told James Russell Lowell, 'which is intelligent and sympathetic, which can understand and stamp what is good and what is bad; we do not write for idiots or for bores; we gather strength from sympathy; we must have our sounding-board to give effect to the tune we play. Allston starved. . . . The sky itself is hard and distant. The heart grows into stone. . . .'

Things were so changed. There was so much to contend with! Had not the Boston Museum refused shyly the Venus by William Page, a 'consummate nude,' offered through subscription by the Americans in Rome? Story viewed with a sinking heart—after Florence—the shingle and clapboard grandeur of Newport. He listened to the talk of dollars in horse-cars. Shoddy and petroleum had raised their heads very high, indeed!

As he thought of his benighted compatriots, an idea occurred that would sum up in allegory all that troubled him: 'I would like to make a bas-relief of the Pied Piper with the children flocking after him. . . .' For were they not all children, in fact, who must be charmed and led by a greater magic? But in the next breath he thought: 'What encouragement to do it? Nobody will buy it. Nobody cares for such things. There would be real interest if I had imported a cargo of saltpetre.'

With an alienated mind, he had found himself steeped in a society both fundamentally and superficially bourgeois. . . . 'Its very virtues irritated him,' says Henry James, 'its ability to be strenuous without passion, its cultivation of its serenity, its presentation of a surface on which the only ruffle was an occasionally acuter spasm of the moral sense.'

The Italianized artist looked with bewilderment at the drastic changes, so notable after long absence, in the values, proportions, interest, dignity, decency, of all the objects once agreeably familiar to him—and then departed for his beloved Rome.

He returned then to pass his long life in the richly colored Roman world, 'the prey of mere beguilement.' There were conversations with distinguished friends, the idolatry of Shakespeare, the imitation of Browning in verse, the long succession of romantic and decorous statues which brought him fame and wealth from England and even America.

In his moderated way he had drunk the cup of the Borgias! It is as if he declared, 'I give up everything for a lifetime of the golden air!' But the golden air reduced the intensity of his art. In such a vaporing mood there could be no single-minded, sustained gathering up of all his faculties for an onslaught. Subjects floated by him in the languid Roman daylight. He expended himself in vague and crowded studies. He dreamed of the great past, whose ruins were all about him, of Antony and Augustus and Cleopatra; above all, in his closing days, of Cleopatra, whom he pictured both in his verse and in his marble. . . .

2

America had become 'a nation of whom the steam-engine is no bad symbol,' wrote Walt Whitman in 1851. The definition is a keen one; and we can scarcely hope to understand the period unless we visualize the lines of steel rail spreading themselves briskly and the little red and black 'iron horses' of the time appearing more and more as the dominant agent of change and reckless growth.

It is by no sentimental or fatuous effort at parable, then, that one may conceive the poet and the artist alike virtually pitted against the steam-engine in a vain contest that could end only in retreat or flight. Two or three years after Whitman's aphorism we find the gifted James Whistler as a young man—utterly confused as to what his career might be—engaged in the almost unthinkable labor of *making locomotives!*

To be sure, with his irrepressible personal charm and most abundant talents he was to become one of the most celebrated painters of the century and to enjoy the most brilliant of careers, for all the wayward course it took. Success, striking effects, came easily to his hand; but it is none the less clear that he was immensely resourceful and not easily to be turned from his purpose. And so we grasp all the better the inevitability of his departure from the native scene, which had so little to teach or humor him with, in order to play upon a larger artistic stage. In the whole record of defections, of the indirect banishment of artistic talent—such as might have furnished life, criticism, direction, excitement in the little American art-world—surely no greater quantity escaped at once and forever than in the case of the young Whistler.

As a child he had received early impressions of the most amazing quarters of the old world. His father, a great military engineer, had carried his family with him from New England to Russia, where he was to build the first railroads for the Czar in the 1840s; and James Whistler had been reared at the court of St. Petersburg like a 'princeling.' He became a queer mixture of Yankee, French, Russian, and even English influences, since his grandfather had been an officer in Burgoyne's army; a world of intrigue, privilege, sophisticated gayety, in which personal charm and address prospered most, stamped itself on his mind.

Repatriated as a boy, at the death of his father,

he was bred to the military career traditional with his family and sent to West Point.

Countless anecdotes cling to the 'witty and paradoxically amusing fellow,' in his youth as in his ripe age—who possessed such an elegant figure, curly black hair, delicate features, soft wild eyes—in short the handsomest and most rakish fellow one might meet in Washington circles. At the Military Academy he had distinguished himself only by his drawings and by his unpardonable breaches of discipline.

He was to have his stupendous career, he was to be talked of, admired, and hated; but now, as if in impatience, the flame of genius burned fitfully and farcically in Whistler.

In 1854, we find him engaged in the locomotive business at Baltimore, where his brothers, in perplexity at his 'flightiness,' sought to set him on his road in the good Yankee manner. They and his mother were alarmed at his taste for drawing. What were they to do about such an unheard-of, such an irresponsible, turn? And so Whistler, perforce, hung about the drafting-rooms of the locomotive shop, sketching wistfully, perhaps Remembrandtesque versions of machines!—since Rembrandt was then his adored idol.

Whistler and the locomotive—what allegory! The locomotive and the railway surely represented the characteristic national effort, the road to power and wealth. Here was the young spark at the very crossroads of destiny, in the early youth of American industry, faced with the chance of becoming one of the grandees of the Gilded Age! But Whistler soon fled from the fierce little iron monsters; incredibly, he wanted 'art,' he wanted conversation, he wanted to be one of the characters he had read of in Murger's *La Vie de Bohème*. . . .

At Washington, near by, he fascinated and amused a portion of the little political and diplomatic world; he employed such frivolous tactics as he may dimly have remembered from the Russian court, as he flitted and fluttered about the balls, receptions, legation dinners, in quest of an official sinecure. Was it simply for the sake of his *beaux yeux* that he was admitted to the Geodetic Survey? He would put pretty little landscapes into the maps he drew; that is, when he appeared at all at his desk. Clearly there was no choice, there was no career for him; and least of all was there the space, the long rope, that his temperament fretfully, uneasily sought.

He might find the Russian Ambassador entertaining for a time. But who was there to guide or instruct him? Where was there his equal or his better, humanly speaking, for sensibility, humor, imagination, in this single-minded bourgeois society? Even twenty years after it would still be the case that a man with disposition or genius for an art was an outcast. MacDowell much later, at the age of fifteen, had reached a point where there was no one in this country who could teach him music, although he thought that he knew very little as yet!

No sooner was Whistler of age and possessed of an annuity than he set off for Paris in all haste, never stopping to look behind him. He was to study painting at the schools and in the Latin Quarter; schools touched him but little, whereas the free and attractive manners of the Quarter delighted his heart. He was a bohemian; he gained many picturesque cronies, 'shirtless' friends, avoiding the Anglo-Saxon students; he drew facile sketches of passers-by on the terraces of cafés, like the irrepressible Gavarni, while loiterers watched and bantered with him. He spent his money gayly and simulated poverty among the little *midinettes* whom he adored, the fakers and *viveurs* of an old Paris which was to pass out with the end of the Second Empire. What an animated, colorful world it was, still in the full flush of romanticism! Under the bright gaslights along the boulevards, the crowds eddied about the theaters and the great cafés of the period, Tortoni's and the Anglais, frequented by the brilliant Manet and the 'open air' painters. For Whistler had begun to make serious friendships, with Legros, Fantin-Latour, Dégas, artists of great talent. Full of an unconquerable impatience and confessing his 'terrible lack of education,' he had begun to work.

He was at this time self-admittedly 'a blackguard swelling with vanity at being able to show the painters his splendid gifts, gifts only requiring a severe training to make their possessor at the present moment a master, and not a perverted pupil.' Yet in his own fashion, through painful and uncertain labor, he acquired this discipline. He became deeply engrossed. There was a legend, instinctively believed, that an American had some mysterious hereditary handicap to overcome before he could pass muster, that he must work ten times as hard as the others, that he had far more to learn. Was it true? Whistler at any rate became a good European. . . . 'There is no nationality in painting,' he declared. With the revolutionary younger painters who surrounded Manet, the later Impressionists, he exhibited in 1863 his famous *White Girl* at the 'Salon of the Rejected Painters,' to which Zola had brought so much polemical notoriety. In the heat of artistic warfare he must have lost track utterly of the great bloody one waged at the very time across the sea.

Ultimately Whistler came to live in London, where he was oriented naturally to the 'advanced' circles of the Pre-Raphaelite painters, who at their banquets revived Keats's toast to the confusion of Newton 'because he had destroyed the poetry of the rainbow.'

In the '70s and '80s painting acquired vague new attributes in the hands of the Impressionists and Pre-Raphaelites. Painters sought the qualities of music in color. Whistler, under the influence of the newly discovered Japanese art and of the French Impressionists, now made *Symphonies*, *Arrangements in Blue and Gold*, *Nocturnes*. . . . There were famous polemics, attacks and counter-attacks, such as the outrageously funny suit of Whistler against Ruskin for the latter's abuse of *Battersea Bridge*. Whistler sought, as he asserted, the 'poetry of painting,' which could 'put form and color into such perfect harmony . . . that exquisiteness is the result.' His painting must stand alone, 'and appeal to the artistic sense of eye or ear, without confounding this with emotions entirely foreign to it, such as devotion, pity, love, patriotism, and the like.'

One wonders what would have happened to such a militant, such an emancipated aesthetic in the fairly void American art-world. What would Whistler have been with no Academy to bombard, no newspapers in which to slate his contemporaries, no Oscar Wildes to engage in a duel of wit?

In Victorian London he was execrated and lionized at once. He marched from success to scandal, from scandal to success. Because of irregularities in his domestic life he might suffer for a time the censure of the Grundies, so that in bitterness he rated his guests lower than Yankees and referred to them always as 'the Islanders.' Yet he knew how to emerge from obloquy by some skillful coup, some one of his toasts or epigrams, that brought again the blaze of publicity which he loved so well. He had always his dangling white lock of hair, his monocle, his metallic, sneering laugh. The sublime dandy knew an amazing vogue and in the end the numerous pupils, the adulation, the legends of a master. His celebrity brought him the attention of his native land and the visitations of artistic pilgrims, but nothing could ever entice him to return to America.

We may tend to appraise his art a little more severely now; we may grant his many experiments only a partial value, wondering especially at the murky vagueness which he preferred, the 'single tones' he sought. Yet it is impossible to deny the intense aesthetic consciousness which he brought to nineteenth century painting, his high gifts for drawing, and, above all, the 'personality,' the intelligence, the worldliness, that he is remembered for.

Whether in France or Italy or his foggy England, certainly it had been a magnificent life in the fullest sense, which at its worst reverses he must never have regretted. He had missed, to be sure, the one chance in a thousand to 'get into' locomotives at the *bon moment*.

3

The absentees, returned to America after a period of years, would look upon a world that they no longer recognized or understood. At the time of the quarrels of the painters in Paris, in which Whistler played such an excellent part, the battle of Gettysburg was decided and the belated industrial revolution, long known to Europe, had come to the United States under the barrage of war. Great movements of population had begun; villages in the east were depopulated; continental railroads spread their network everywhere. And while fortunes changed hands in a frenzy of speculation during the hurried partition of the vast Federal domain, while new alignments of wealth and poverty were fixed, the nation was given up to the anarchy of growth and multiplication, the whole continent was shaken 'from axis to periphery.'

The old industrial elements had been agriculture, handwork, and to a large degree learning. They had been superseded by great mechanical energies: coal, iron, steam. The latent forces, long in preparation, had been roused to an incredible pitch by the turmoil and bravura of war. A new economy had triumphed over the ancient feudal one; slavery had been stamped out, but had freedom been gained? The tendency to consolidation, the 'new national unity,' was in force, overcoming the individualism of regions and submerging all their traditions and forms of life.

In the face of such social upheavals—so different from the merely political ones of 1776—one would have expected that efforts of statesmanship would be exerted toward a social program, that ultimate human ends and values would be consulted in the crisis. Nothing of the kind. A veritable jungle period was initiated in which anonymous giants or adventurers of fortune contributed to the national expansion without major disasters, merely by grasping at their opportunities. The whole continental empire was constructed from below, while an older political leadership was thrust aside; the régime of the Commodore Vanderbilts, the Jay Goulds, and the Jim Fisks, nullified that of doctrinaires and orators and moralists who belonged to the eighteenth century.

It is valuable, at this point, to consider the confusion of enlightened New England. For the new order the philosophers of Concord, who lived on, superannuated, in a nimbus of inexplicable literary glory, had no message, no leadership. They had nothing in fact but their sense of deception—if they would confess it—and their impotence. They had labored for the 'good war,' as Emerson had called it, and in the interests of Abolition. But the stake that had been won was a protective tariff!

Besides, the region which had promised most for civilization had entered upon its economic decline. As the energies of the nation rushed pell-mell westward to build new cities at railway junctions, the center of wealth shifted far off toward coal and oil fields. Here in the new cohesions of population, none spoke of principles; no one remembered any longer why the war had been fought.

And now it emerges how the prophecies of Concord had been unfounded and misleading to extremes. They had been libertarians without a program; they had urged individualism when the world about them and all its opportunities clamored for unity and, in fact, uniformity. Their vision of a democratic society was one founded upon agriculture; but you could not stay the avalanche. Under the loose institutions, in the turmoil and pullulation of democracy, industry prospered rather than the human arts which they longed for.

It seems more and more like madness to have preached individualism, of all creeds, to a society whose members stared at Eldorados in oil, steel, coal, to be had for the mere ruthless grasping. And to have added the immunity of blessed democratic institutions, which freed the irresponsible adventurer from all restraint or reprisal in the name of the collective good, seems more madness still.

Of what avail was the 'rude sincerity' of which Thoreau had offered the example by cooking his own food and refusing to wear neckties? The anarchism of Jay Gould was more powerful and prevailed. Nor had the 'independence' which Emerson urged helped much in the face of an imperious economy which flung men under the regimen of the new barons and gathered 'Roman mobs' in industrial cities. No, there had been no program which envisaged the actualities of the approaching society. And besides, the individualism of Emerson was of a kind that was too lacking in rudeness, ill-nature, too full of gentle amiabilities and tolerances. One left him in despair at a naïveté that would circumvent human lusts and physical laws by an appeal to the spiritual faculties.

The generation that had arisen during the Civil War learned to renounce New England, which had been so religious while hating the churches, which had rejected the ways of living of other men while having none to offer in their stead.

'My memory speaks to me,' says Henry James, 'of the Concord school rather as of a supreme artless word on the part of the old social order than as a charged intimation or announcement on the part of the new.' And Mark Twain had exclaimed more crudely that Emerson and Dr. Holmes at a banquet made him feel 'like a barkeeper in Heaven.'

But even the *illuminati* who had lived in the Brook Farm community and written for *The Dial* seemed to repent now of their early ways. 'How surprised,' wrote one of them, 'would some of those [*Dial*] writers be, if they should in prosaic days read what they then wrote under the spell of that fine frenzy!' And another wrote: 'We have found "realizing the ideal" to be impracticable in proportion as the ideal is raised high. But "idealizing the real" is not only practicable but the main secret of the art of living.' [3]

The sense for us of such melancholy recantations is of a promising intellectual movement aborted. Once

[3] Cited by Lewis Mumford. *The Golden Day,* New York, 1926.

the Brahmins had passed, they had no successors whatsoever by whom their peculiar functions might be carried on.

Indeed, literature and idealism now passed into the hands of women, as Mr. Van Wyck Brooks notes: 'But unlike those of France—sad ubiquitous spinsters, left behind with their own desiccated souls by the stampede of the young men westward.' New England had retained its 'culture' by default, and the New England spinster with her narrow experience, her complex of repressions, and all her glacial taboos of good form had become the arbiter of art and manners!

Of this decadent residue from the period of 'plain living and high thinking' Henry James has drawn a cruel picture in *The Bostonians.* One may well be terrified by the procession of resolute, fanatical maids, the apostles of feminism and mesmerism, who fill the scene. It is all 'a feminine, a nervous, a hysterical, chattering, canting age; an age of hollow phrases and false delicacy and exaggerated solicitudes and coddled sensibilities.' And how remote New England seems now from the pulse of American life! The remedies and cults in vogue become as absurd as the bonnets once in fashion.

The dismay and the confusion of the New England bourgeois is not to be laughed at. Their undoing signified clearly the transference of wealth, and likewise of power, to new unknown hands—the dissolution of a nucleus which had secretly ruled the Republic more or less since the eighteenth century. A realistic notion of democracy might even hold paradoxically that the existence of such a class, with its association of 'talent and wealth' (and its disinterested offshoots, to whom wealth was meaningless), was the only safeguard for free institutions and loose government.

At any rate they were undone on the eve of President Grant's first administration; and the autobiography of Henry Adams, scion of just such a New England family as had played a dominant rôle in the affairs of the Republic, offers the most eloquent and pathetic testimony of the transition.

He describes—and it is highly significant—how on a hot July night of 1868, the Adams family and the Motley family arrived in New York, after many years of distinguished service to the state in foreign lands. And Henry Adams, a young man of merely literary and political tastes, voices his wonder and stupefaction.

'Had they been Tyrian traders of the year 1000 B.C., landing from a galley fresh from Gibraltar,' he writes in *The Education*, 'they could hardly have been stranger on the shore of a world so changed from what it had been ten years before.'

Adams had trusted ingenuously in the endurance of the older order. In accordance with the Adams tradition his father had gone to London as ambassador and devoted his human and political arts to preventing England from interceding in the war. Henry Adams had labored under him in London. He had toured Italy, and like Gibbon had 'sat in the ruins of the Capitol at evening,' contemplating his future destiny. And now in peace time, after long absence, he could perceive the magnitude of the revolution which had taken place.

His world was dead, he felt. 'The result of this revolution upon a survivor from the '50s resembled the action of the earthworm; he could no longer see his own trail; he had become an estray; a flotsam or jetsam of wreckage; a belated reveler, or scholar-gypsy like Matthew Arnold. His father and Motley—all were equally survivals from the forties—bric-à-brac from the time of Louis Philippe; doctrinaires; ornaments that had been more or less suited to the colonial architecture. . . . They could scarcely have earned five dollars a day in modern industry.'

His perplexity was very great. What was a young man to do, a young man who had been bred to the belief that learning and good connections would prepare him for the public service? He was 'educated labor' and by that token inferior to the veriest Irish peasant or Polish Jew from Cracow. Above all he must abandon literature, and for that matter, politics. His brother, Charles Francis Adams, wisely determined to strike for the railroads. (Ultimately he became president of a great railroad; but we know from his own confession that he was unhappy and despised his colleagues, whom he hoped he would not have to meet or converse with again even in Heaven!)

'The New Americans,' Henry Adams reflected, 'must create a world of their own . . . where they had not yet created a road or even learned to dig their own iron. *They had no time for thought.* They saw and could see nothing beyond their day's work; their attitude toward the universe outside was that of the deep-sea fish. Above all they naturally and intensely disliked to be told what to do and how to do it, by men who took their ideas and methods from the abstract theories of history, philosophy, or theology.'

On the new scale of power, merely to make the continent habitable would require an outlay that would have bankrupted the world. The field was vast, altogether beyond control or calculation; and society dropped every thought save that single fraction called a railway system. This would require the energies of a generation. . . .

The key to the situation is given in Henry Adams' statement: '*The generation between 1865 and 1895 was already mortgaged to the railways, and no one knew it better than the generation itself.*'

III

THE EDUCATION OF HENRY JAMES

> *The inward drama of this perception on the part of the repatriated pilgrim . . . has never been noted, reported, commemorated, in a manner worthy of its intrinsic interest.*—HENRY JAMES.

'IS ONE'S only safety, then, in flight? . . .' This is the question which we find the young Henry James putting to himself in those post-bellum days which have assumed for us the qualities of an all but disastrous transition. It is the question which the conscience of the whole generation faces; and since it is Henry James who articulates it best, who sleeps with it, walks with it over a long period of years, and answers it—so that all the gradual steps in the 'process of a foredoomed detachment' may be followed—he becomes simply the central figure in the drama that is played under the strenuous surface, the character who illuminates most strongly the problems approached here.

There are indeed many reasons why we should devote our largest interest, the foreground of our picture, to this man who lived above all by his concept of civilization, whose whole career was a quarrel with—if not barbarism, then—provincialism. He is not an *obvious* hero; he is one of those great heroes of art, however, whose whole adventure, involving the sacrifice of everything else, of family, sex, country even, has been that of the conquest of his art. Modern criticism, after long neglect, must eventually accord him a very high place, probably as the greatest American novelist of his time, and one who even among all his contemporaries, internationally, seems peculiarly close to the aspirations of twentieth century literature. But what concerns us most here, for the sake of our problem, is his keen awareness of his American environment and his response to it. We are struck by his early resolution to become an artist, his efforts to perfect himself, his long education elaborately planned, and the subsequent spiritual suffering which this produced in the light of hostile native conditions. We may follow the various stages of his deliberation, as between cultivating himself in the United States or in Europe, up to his final choice and his apostasy—for it was apostasy that he committed; it was an abandonment of that Americanism, that folk-religion which defines itself so harshly in the second half of the nineteenth century, for the sake of his finer view of civilization. The older, richer continent would become his Great Good Place, where he might practice such a faith more feasibly; and if in the end he is to be undeceived and disillusioned, are the needs which drove him upon his search and his pilgrimage in any way the less significant or imperative?

For Henry James, as for his brother William, the boyhood interval in Europe of four or five years, the schooling at Geneva, at Boulogne-sur-Mer, the wandering through Paris and London, had made a deep, a strategic, impression. Dressed in the high black hats and inveterate gloves of the fashion, in a state of the 'direst propriety,' they had moved and stared about while Henry James had felt (though in retrospect, long after) 'the rich burden of a Past, the consequence of too much history, almost. . . .' In the gray street-scene, in the curious old manners, tones, obsequiosities, 'the great dim social complexity' of Europe seemed to mass itself, the order, the harmony, disclosed. And in Paris the old buildings along the river, clear-faced, straight-standing, had seemed to utter a message which expressed their style, as if: 'Yes, small staring *jeune homme*, we are dignity, and memory, and measure, we are conscience and proportion and taste. . . .' And the Louvre had been like a vast, deafening, reverberant chorus, 'an endless golden riot—history, fame and power—the world raised to the richest and noblest expression.'

He had, in short, taken to Europe with unnatural precocity, just as the sense of ugliness had awakened too early in him, with the result that he was to languish for 'the nostalgic cup' during the long American years intervening before new peregrinations.

The extraordinary education of the James children, along the plan set by that great 'mandarin,' Henry James, Sr., had then proceeded in the more leisurely and ample society of Newport. Newport, with its admixture of senators and financiers, artists and foreigners, lay among the *parages* of culture. 'It had the best of the Parisian and the New England accent.' Elsewhere one's American consciousness might be starved, but surely not in Newport—'for our Newport, even during the War, lived mainly and quite visibly by the opera-glass, and was comparatively, and in its degree, cosmopolite.'

In the circle of their father's friends, and under the tutelage of Hunt and John Lafarge (for William James prepared himself to become a painter), it was as if they were sheltered from the barbarous world without their microcosm. Here one felt the felicity of personal and social experience; one responded to the 'literary and artistic,' even the romantic. One felt the triumph of human values here, even though they assumed a virtually *missionary* character, under the circumstances. Such a missionary as William Hunt was felt to be from top to toe the living and communicating Artist. The master's house, where Henry, too, daubed at drawing-blocks, was in itself a rounded and satisfying world, encircled by many trees, and excluding such 'vulgar' sounds, false notes, and harsh reminders, as were elsewhere known. And the fascinating John Lafarge, through his long residence abroad, his foreign connections, his charm, appeared a rare original, superbly a man of the world through the enrichments of curiosity, taste, talent, while not lacking, either, the elements of the dandy and the cavalier.

It was Lafarge who introduced them in their happy adolescence to the poems of Browning, even to the profuse and adumbrated Balzac. And there was notably the influence of Ruskin, and in the conversation of their father much consideration of Fourier and his great plan for regenerating the world. William James now adventurously seized upon the volumes of the daring Renan or Schopenhauer, whose ideas he espoused with a zeal for such things which was soon to overshadow his interest in the plastic arts.

Nor were Henry James's notions of his talents more than vague as yet. Secretly it was for literature that he prepared himself. His family held that he was addicted to the reading of too many novels. From the first he had been absorbing with passionate, informed attention his Thackeray and George Eliot; and in the *Revue des Deux Mondes* he followed much the frequent studies in moral customs, the portraits of the 'blue-chinned, corrupt *larbin*, and the smart *soubrette*.' The critical sense was strong in him, so that he read nothing without perceiving the method and the form. By his knowledge chiefly of the masters' secrets, wrested from their works, the bookish young man aspired to become one of the great novelists.

And so, living afloat and disconnected from the more violent currents, within the mild Newport colony, he was permitted by his parent to approach life slowly, warned of 'materialism,' and urged on to a career of a more generous order. But was he given any guarantee that such a position would be at all tenable or feasible on the 'dark continent' where one either made money or got tipsy? Was not Mr. James, by his very liberality, ruining his sons' chances to become decent American citizens during the approaching decades? They were educated in the light of liberties and refinements of an older order, where they should have been hardened to face an Iron Age.

2

The Civil War came 'like a thief in the night' upon this remote and finely conscious group. In the disarray and revolution, a society was foundering at last. The strange, expressionless recruits marched in regiments toward the front, without enthusiasm.[1] The two younger brothers, more adequate physically and with stronger conviction, volunteered, while William and Henry James remained at a Harvard that had grown dull and comfortless. During these days of *Sturm und Drang*, no matter who won, a

[1] More sensitive chroniclers such as H. Adams, Bierce, and Henry James attest to the apathy on the part of northern and southern masses alike.

sense of defeat or even failure hung over them. William James, now a devoted pupil of the inspiring Agassiz, became a man of 'science,' while his conscience underwent the first painful struggles with agnosticism. Henry read Blackstone in the dreary little Law College and lived passively through the languishing interval during which he felt his young life 'to have been made bitter, under appearances of smug accommodation, by too prompt a mouthful of the fruit of the tree of knowledge.'

Wilkie James returned one day, so shattered that some years after the war he expired of his wounds. The war which killed his brother, and a series of misfortunes which overtook cherished relatives, fixed in Henry James a sense of surrounding violence and instability beyond the family hearth. What was to be witnessed all round them but ferryboats going up in flames with all their passengers consumed, horrendous railroad accidents, bloody battles, riotous elections, panics? The chronicle of his own family was one of early deaths, suicides, arrested careers, broken promises, orphaned children. He would recall for a long time after the members of the dying family, weak or fortunate in their time, grandees or crazed adventurers, to whose aid his father had often come. He remembered visiting, on a dusky wintry Sunday in New York, the house of his uncle, Robertson Walsh, 'where the hapless younger brother lay dying . . . amid odours of tobacco and drugs.'

There had been no *mean*, least of all the golden one, since it was the want or the possession of gold which precipitated catastrophe. It was very well for his father and the men of Concord to have floated in the 'high optimistic tradition' which believed in an imminent improvement in human affairs; an old society, an old order, had vanished into the past, and the new, 'barren of romance and of grace,' as he reflected, offered the most menacing conditions, full of pitfalls and looming disasters. 'Languid or brooding, morose or anxiously mute,' he recalls himself, in the subdued Cambridge world of the late '60s.

In those days an old-fashioned shabbiness and jollity lingered about Boston and Cambridge: there was the same dismal wealth, the same speechifying, the same anxious respectability. The local orators and poets brimmed with jokes and conventional sentiments; the same tinkling horse-car jogged its half-hour to Boston, carrying the packed passengers to the delights of female society, the theater, a good dinner.

'It was an idyllic, haphazard, humoristic existence,' Santayana tells us, 'without fine imagination, without any familiar infusion of scholarship, without articulate religion: a flutter of intelligence in the void, flying into trivial play, only to drop back into the drudgery of affairs. There was the love of beauty, but without the sight of it; for the bits of pleasant landscape or the works of art which might break the ugliness of the foreground were a sort of aesthetic miscellany, enjoyed as one enjoys a museum.'

The legend of culture adhered to Cambridge, just as the tradition of intellectual leadership still clung to a more conservative, more materialistic Harvard. But the literature of the years immediately following the Civil War offered nothing but swan-songs: the last words of Concord, such as Emerson's *Terminus*, and the mere translations of Longfellow, Bayard Taylor, Norton, Bryant, and Cranch. During the next decades everything that New England did represented a 'genteel,' mildly missionary labor that had curiously lost touch with the life of the nation. The effect was likely to be deadly upon a young man now bristling with artistic curiosity and venturesomeness.

Henry James made literary associations, whose hold upon him, however, was not to be strong. There was Professor Charles Eliot Norton, who translated Dante, championed Ruskin and the Italian painters, and edited the *North American Review;* he had read Henry James's earliest stories and counseled him to abandon the law. Norton presided in these days as a 'representative of culture,' and his hereditary home at Shady Hill suggested life in an older and more polished society; it had rich spoils, in the shape of pictures, books, drawings, medals, relics; it had the atmosphere of Europe, with which Norton through long visits to Italy and England had formed many ties and friendships. It was through Norton that James met Howells and as a result saw his prose admitted to the *Atlantic Monthly*.

The two younger men became fast friends. 'We were of like Latin sympathies,' Howells says. 'James was inveterately and intensely French; with the use of three or four years of life in Italy, we could make him feel that we met on common ground. He could not always keep his French background back, and sometimes he wrote English that was easily convicted of Gallicism; but this was in the helplessness of early use and habit from his life and school in France throughout boyhood.'

Henry James had only lived for four years in France and Switzerland; yet he drew largely on this period, and his early stories are filled with châteaux and picturesque peasants and abducted heroines. They are precious; they have a certain sprightliness and wit, without substance; their irony is that of a young man who has enjoyed thus far being rejected by ladies whom he courts without conviction. The style is simple, save for occasional flights, at his twenty-fifth year, toward the sententious and the romantic.

'We seemed presently to be always meeting together, and always talking of methods of fiction,' Howells relates. And he adds, 'I was seven years older, but I was much his junior in the art we both admired.'

They had 'tremendous talks,' pacing up and down among the fallen leaves during the chill autumn nights, while they discovered to themselves 'the true principles of literary art.' They were gripped by large ambitions; James's technical sophistication was astonishing, and his critical sense, his knowledge of everything that was being written or tried by his contemporaries, was no less impressive. These two young men were perhaps the only ones who were then consciously preparing themselves, by long exercise and reflection, for the novel, for the phantom even of the Great American Novel, which so dangled before literary minds. 'Realism' was in the air; it was felt in the polemics of the *Revue des Deux Mondes;* it arose from the pages of the heroic George Eliot and the admired Thackeray. And the idea that weighed upon James with utter fascination was that of a great American *Comédie Humaine*, which could be constructed perhaps out of the very disastrous lives of those interesting uncles and cousins of his own family, whom he seemed always to have been scanning with such a purpose in his eye. The communings of the two young writers had been an excitement; and in his delight over their friendship, Howells had written impulsively to a friend how 'earnest' James was, and how extremely gifted—'gifted enough to do better than any one has yet done toward making us a real American novel.'

Though editors like Howells and Norton and Godkin of *The Nation* accepted James's reviews and stories eagerly, the public demurred. 'People were very much struck with his work—but mostly not pleased with it,' an editor related. And by 1867, Howells noted that although he found James's stories admirable and having every element of artistic success, he no longer felt sure of the public. Poor James, he thought, must in a great degree *create his own audience.*

The popular taste of the time had expressed itself overwhelmingly for novels of local color and native humor. The fabulous success of Mark Twain and Bret Harte overshadowed all other literary events. With this taste the remoter fiction of Henry James came in conflict. Everything had conspired to form him as something of an exquisite, an aesthete, for whom the demands of art were imperative, rather than the taste of the public in the matter. But the indifference, the voiced hostility, of his public served at any rate to intensify his detachment, without making him lower his colors. The public, when he thought of it, emphasized his ennui, and hastened the process of alienation.

He was to issue with facility and urbanity a long series of reviews, stories, travel-sketches, valued by the *illuminati;* but for a dozen or more years after his début he was to remain in an agonizing uncertainty as to his place in the social scheme.[2]

He came to be tormented by, to be even ashamed of, his environment! He was himself steeped, as he says of William Story, 'with alienated mind, in a society both fundamentally and superficially bourgeois.' Above all he could draw from this innocent society neither the stimulus nor the material for the fictions he proposed to write.

'It takes so many *things*,' he said later of the case of Hawthorne, 'it takes such an accumulation of history and custom, such a complexity of manners and types to form a fund of suggestion for a novelist. . . .' These *things*, these items of civilization, as he defined them, were so lamentably lacking in the thinly composed American society. There was no aristocracy, no clergy, no class of country gentlemen, no political society, no sporting class. . . . How could one characterize, how could one *satirize*, like Thackeray, a people whose shifting movements could be placed against no backdrop of traditions or conventions, since they hadn't any, and neither opposed nor accepted them!

2 It must be noted that writing and the fine arts were widely encouraged and rewarded, then as now: i.e. as professional pursuits, as practical tasks and a kind of business. What the American mind could not tolerate, and regarded as academic luxuries, fit only to amuse the ladies, as Santayana observes in *Character and Opinion in the United States,* was generous execution, 'all those little sacrifices to instinct and custom, which we call grace . . . that diffused charm which qualifies all human action where men are artists by nature.'

And so, with the example of Thackeray notably in mind, our young novelist hunted inconsolably among the purlieus of the rich in Newport and wandered even to Saratoga, where a strange, flashy sporting and profiteering class reared itself in the big wooden hotels—in search of 'items of civilization. . . .'

Nor did the little metropolis of Boston and its 'brilliant' suburbs yield the materials he sought. The sympathy of men like Norton and of Howells—a converted New Englander—may have counted for much; but in the end he felt only revulsion against the New England spirit. In the ordered and materialistic universe which men had begun to construct after Darwin and Herbert Spencer, one questioned bitterly the superior piety and optimism of the Transcendentalists. A mood of pessimism weighed over his generation. 'I can't bring myself,' his brother William had exclaimed in a crisis of conscience, 'to blink the evil out of sight and gloss it over, as so many other men are able to. It's as real as the good, and if it's denied, good must be denied too. . . . It seems to me that all a man has to depend on in this world, is, in the last resort, mere brute power of resistance.'

New England had lived only for moral consolations, and the relations of men were lacking in intimacy or complexity—the only intimate relation was in fact that of a man's fireside—his intimacy with his wife, his children, his Creator. The others, the outside ones, remained, formal, civil, dutiful, but never could become easy without appearing to become frivolous.

How 'pale and thin' Emerson's life had been! Henry James drew clear lessons from his elders. For his part, he had always felt himself 'in New England, *but not of it.*' With his passion for craftsmanship, for style, he desired a longer rope; he desired the right to lose himself in his curiosities, in sensuous experiences, to saturate himself with the beautiful—oh, mildly, mildly, to be sure, with many Victorian reservations! But none the less did he feel himself liberated from moral dogmas; while the mere life of art which he visioned, the quest of civilization, came more and more to seem something 'frivolous' or 'dissipated' and at once infinitely adored and desirable the more it was condemned.

Poor Charles Norton would find his life of effort to brand the ugly and the inferior wherever he found them vain, vain! 'His life was to be a compromise,' James surmised as he removed himself from Norton's fraternal wing. This most liberally emancipated and initiated son of the Puritans was to plead for style while clinging to substance, to try to 'lose himself in the labyrinth of delight while keeping tight hold of the clew of duty; to address himself to the moral conscience while speaking ostensibly for imagination and free curiosity.' Norton was to find, in short, that the New England air was no conductor of any appeal to an aesthetic aim.

And of Howells, James felt secret misgivings too. Did Howells, after all, possess the kind of imagination necessary to compose the broad exhaustive record of American *mœurs* which James bided his time to write?

If James foresaw, as he actually did, the failure of his friends, he was no less aware of the peril of his own situation, and no less destined to suffer under the steadily enlarging sense of his own futility. Disaffection and ennui massed themselves, and the strange obsession grew upon him of his particular quarrel with his American environment.

He was a man who was meant surely to ornament his land; training, education, exposure to humanizing influences, had shaped him for this. Doubtless the country needed ornament, needed it badly, as Henry Adams observed; but it needed energy and capital still more. The great men of the time, the folk-heroes, such as General Grant or Jay Gould or Vanderbilt, were as a rule not ornamental and lacked social charm almost as much as they lacked social purpose. . . . So that James inevitably must have seen his hands busied for long years, not with perfecting his art, but in the sheer *making of a place for it*. He would have to be spokesman and apologist for the rights of the individual under the rule of the mob, for the cultivation of the human graces and refinements which vanished under the mounting ugliness of the industrial society; his writings must be filled with indignant outcries against the preëmptions of the Kings of Bathtubs and the Kings of Coal, Oil, Steel, or Lumber.

For the artist must needs justify his apostasy. In earlier times, classical or mediaeval, the instinctive union of religious and social impulses may have produced happy artists whose handiworks took their place naturally in the life of the race, naturally and unquestioningly as they were conceived. But now there was a great and strange dissociation, a schism between the life of art and the life of men. The objects of art were assembled and ranged like so many curios in the museums of a democratic era. For all living purposes they had the value of dead things, and as proof of this there was the American notion that a great artist or a great poet must be dead first.

There was something pathetically remote and eclectic in the way John Lafarge made stained-glass windows in an age whose most characteristic architecture would be the skyscraper, the factory, and the warehouse. Lafarge's thirteenth century medium was divorced functionally from contemporary realities; but no less was the prose of Henry James divorced. One could look forward safely to a time when the honest triumph of democratic masses would obliterate all those arts, plastic and reflective, derived from primitive, feudal, or aristocratic ages. The only hope would reside in the emergence elsewhere of the instinct for play and ornament in new guises, shaped by new crafts and new values. The façade of a bootshop would answer for the stained-glass window, the Movietone for the introspections of the profound novelist of souls. . . . But the intellectual generation of the late nineteenth century clung desperately still, as a little band of the disaffected, the alienated, and the esoteric, to the notion of a humanism which would cultivate and protect the arts.

Nor is the accent of the 'missionary' lacking from the early writings of Henry James. From 1870 to 1885 his books would be filled with his message of dissent, burdened, as it were, with the justifying of his place under the sun. (It was only long after, in a distant land, when he had long separated himself, long abandoned hope for betterment either of the world or of his own situation in it, that he became a very great and self-sufficient artist.)

The American as artist, or as the pilgrim of culture, would be the dominant theme of James's earlier writings. The flame smolders, too, in the American, but it is never 'fanned by the breath of criticism,' he says in *Roderick Hudson*. 'He sees nothing, hears nothing to help him to self-knowledge. He's hopelessly discontented, but doesn't know where to look for help. . . .' He is alone, misplaced, exposed to ridicule or extinction. And James, like his Roderick Hudson, must have cried out often at the anomaly of isolation:

'It's a wretched business, this practical quarrel of ours with our own country, this everlasting impatience to get out of it. Is one's only safety then in flight? This is an American day, an American landscape, an American atmosphere. It certainly has its merits, and some day when I'm shivering with ague in classic Italy, I shall accuse myself of having slighted them.'

The goal, the Great Good Place toward which Henry James pined from Cambridge, was of course Europe, the deep, dark, rich old world; and toward the end of 1868, our 'morose or anxiously mute' young man notes in a letter that a journey to Europe has 'ceased to look positively and aggressively impossible.' And moving swiftly now upon this determination, he is enabled soon after to view the arrival of the English springtime from the docks of Liverpool!

3

An intense excitement, jubilation, now grips him. He is no longer languid or brooding; he babbles wildly and beautifully, even 'hysterically,' as he would say later, of his poignant hour.

Henry James worked up, in somewhat subjective and factitious fashion, a little romance or legend which lends dramatic and even historical significance to his flight. He is figuratively a soldier or leader in the small army of the 'few real fugitives from the rule of the mob'; he is, simply, the Passionate Pilgrim incarnate. A considerable portion of his generation, as he imagines it, has caught badly 'the Great American disease'—the appetite, morbid and monstrous, for colors and form, for the picturesque and the romantic at any price. Did they come into the world with it, with the germs implanted, or antecedent to experience? Did they catch it early? At any rate, once here, they feel as they look about that they are going 'to save their souls, or at least their senses.'

'We're like travelers in the desert—' he exclaims, 'deprived of water and subject to the terrible mirage, the torment of illusion, of the thirst-fever. They hear the splash of fountains, they see green gardens and orchards that are hundreds of miles away. So we with *our* thirst—except that it's more wonderful; we have before us the beautiful old things we've never seen at all, and when we do at last see them—if we're lucky! —we simply recognize them. What experience does is merely to confirm and consecrate our confident dream.'

Henry James stopped in an old inn in Half-Moon Street on his arrival in London. No sooner had he crossed the threshold of this retreat than he felt, as one of his earliest characters says, that he had cut 'a golden-ripe crop of English impressions.' 'I had never before had to do with an eating-house, and had not yet seen the little old English world of Dickens, let alone the ever-haunting one of Hogarth, of Smollett, and of Boswell, drenched with such a flood of light.'

The coffee-room of the Red Lion seemed to have been waiting for him for long years. He had seen it at home, in books; in visions he had wandered about Johnson's London, near Temple Bar. . . . Every face here was a documentary scrap; every sound was strong, whether rich and fine, or only queer and coarse; 'everything in this order drew a positive sweetness from never being—whatever else it was—gracelessly flat.'

He had felt the inconceivable immensity of London. 'The place sits on you, broods on you, stamps on you, with the feet of its myriad bipeds and quadrupeds.' And from his lodgings in Half-Moon Street he had the turmoil of the West End at his elbow, Piccadilly, Park Lane, St. James's Street, all within range of a five-minute stroll. He plunged into this vortex with incredible gusto, 'knocking about in a quiet way and deeply enjoying my little adventure. . . .'

But above the vast dingy expanse of London, with its old towers and palaces, there existed for him already a cultivated society of brilliant men and women, to which he had fortunately been introduced. Exceedingly shy and reserved, he had been led by the Nortons to meet Ruskin and hear him lecture; he had met the marvelous George Eliot; he had lunched with Miss Dickens—in black silk and black lace; he had been taken to the house of Mr. William Morris, filled with the products of his mediaeval craft, stained glass, tiles, tapestry, altar cloths, and in fine everything quaint, archaic, Pre-Raphaelite, and exquisite. And his wife aided him in his labors. 'Oh, *ma chère*, such a wife! *Je n'en reviens pas*—she haunts me still! . . . A figure out of one of Rossetti's pictures; a tall slender woman, in a long dress of some dead purple stuff, *without hoops*, her dark hair falling in great waves about her pale face, out of which the "deep dark strange, sad Swinburnian eyes" loomed at one.'

In short he had been dazzled, although interspersed among his ravings are notes of precocious critical observation. 'Ruskin . . . has been scared back by the grim face of reality into the world of unreason and illusion, and wanders there without a compass and a guide.' Morris, short, burly, corpulent, 'is saved by a perfectly healthy body and temper. . . .'

Henry James kept even a gift for comparisons. His fellow Englishmen at the sanitarium of Malvern had little eye for the things he found delightful in the lovely countryside. They lived wholly in the realm 'of the cut and dried.' But the Americans one met abroad, as he wrote to his brother William, were incredibly worse. 'There is but one word to use in regard to them—vulgar—vulgar—vulgar. Their ignorance—their stingy, defiant, grudging attitude toward everything European—their perpetual reference of all things to some American standard or precedent which exists only in their own unscrupulous windbags—and then our unhappy poverty of voice and speech—these things glare at you hideously.'

Europe, then as now, was an excellent vantage-point from which to study American character. All the reminiscences of historians and philosophers substantiate Henry James's studies of the American in the international scene. Bored, patient, helpless, pathetically dependent on his wife and daughter, Henry Adams resumes, 'the American was to be met at every railway station in Europe, carefully explaining to every listener that the happiest day of his life would be the day he should land on the pier in New York. He was ashamed to be amused; his mind no longer answered to the stimulus of variety; he could not face a new thought. All his immense strength, his intense nervous energy, his keen analytic perception, were oriented in one direction, and he could not change it.' And the American character which showed itself so clearly at Washington—as in Lincoln, quiet, peaceful, shy, tragic, or in Grant, inarticulate, uncertain, distrustful, awed by money—knew how to amuse itself at home. Excessive work, excessive whiskey and cards. . . .

'We seem a people of *character*,' James observed to his brother; 'we seem to have energy, capacity, and intellectual stuff in ample measure. What I have pointed out as our vices are *the elements of the modern man with culture left out*. It's the absolute and incredible lack of *culture* that strikes you in common traveling Americans.' The excellence of the English on the other hand came from their having been dipped into the great common crucible which gives them 'a sort of coating of comely varnish and color. They have been smoothed and polished by mutual social attrition. They have manners and a language. We lack both, but particularly the latter.'

Ill and alone, Henry James wandered to Oxford and raved of her supreme gratifications, 'the most dignified and most educated of the cradles of our race.' He had seen the great Cathedral tower, high and square, rise far up toward the cloud-dappled blue, and 'tasted deeply of the peculiar stillness and repose of the close.' He had studied the image of the great pile reflected in the yellow Severn; and he had stood wondering 'as to the effect on a man's mind of having in one's boyhood haunted the Cathedral shade as a King's scholar, and yet kept ruddy with much cricket in misty meadows by the Severn.' He had scanned the great green landscape of the downs, haunted by the vague traditions of battles. He had saturated himself, as he wrote to his father, 'in the deepest British picturesque,' and known himself greatly stirred; he was simply taking the adventure of his twenty-sixth year 'hard.'

The Passionate Pilgrim is the title of a story written in 1870 during the youthful *Wanderjahr*. James, who suppressed so much of his youthful writing, preserved this largely for a certain 'documentary and consolatory' character which it clearly contains for us.

Clement Searles has sailed for England. He had learned that he was of old English lineage and inheritor of a sixteenth century manor house, the claim for which is disputed. The great rooms of this country house are full, naturally, of the 'spoils' of the ages—Van Dykes, Rembrandts, Gainsboroughs, magnificent candelabra, majolica—and the American feels for their presence and for the ancient family seat an awakened love that must be bred in his blood. His words are charged with the nostalgia of the youthful James.

'I had the love of old forms and pleasant rites,' he says, 'and I found them nowhere—found a world all hard lines and harsh lights, without shade, without composition, as they say of pictures, without the lovely mystery of color. . . . Sitting here in this old park, in this old country, I feel that I have been on the misty verge of what I might have been! I should have been born here and not there; here my makeshift distinctions would have found things they'd have been true of. . . .'

4

But Italy was the never-to-be-forgotten thrill! James had made a little Swiss tour and crossed the Alps into Venice. And now he sees no one, talks to no one, virtually abandoning himself to his wanderings. His accent grows passionate and jubilant again.

He had arrived in Florence late at night, but instead of going vulgarly to bed he roamed about in the moonlight, viewing for the first time in the shadows of the old square Michael's *David* and Benvenuto's *Perseus!*

We may take again a passage from an early story, *The Madonna of the Future* (1871), in which the errant American exquisite pours out his nostalgia in an outburst of pardonable romanticism: 'The past hovers about like a dream made visible. Fancy the old Florentines strolling up in couples to pass judgment on the last performance of Michael or Benvenuto! The plainest burgher of them all, in his cap and gown, had a taste for the matter. That was the prime of art. . . . The sun stood in his heaven, and his broad and equal blaze made the darkest places bright and the dullest eyes clear. We live in the evening of time. We grope in the gray dusk, carrying each our poor little taper of selfish and painful wisdom, holding it up to the great models and the dim idea and seeing nothing but overwhelming greatness and dimness. The days of illumination are gone—'

And forty years later he marked with feeling the lines devoted to the view from the old church of San Miniato on one of the hills overlooking Florence. The full domes and slender towers of Florence, seen from this terrace, are held 'within the blue sweep of the cup of mountains . . . like the choicest handful of the spoils of time, stored away for keeping.'

How vulgar the world was, outside of Italy! It behooved him then, he told Professor Norton, as a luckless American, 'diabolically tempted of the shallow and superficial,' for once to catch the flavor of an old civilization.

It was in Rome that this flavor was most voluminously received. He grows positively lyrical and tumultuous now in the letters to brother William, who toils in the biological laboratories of Cambridge. He rushes from his hotel, unable to wait for breakfast; from midday to dusk he roams the streets, 'reeling and moaning in a fever of enjoyment.' He has glimpsed the Forum, the Coliseum (*stupendissimo!*), the Pantheon, the Capitol, St. Peter's, the Castle of San Angelo—all the piazzas and ruins and monuments. He has seen St. Peter's filled with foreign ecclesiastics—great armies encamped in prayer on the marble plains of its pavement. He has seen His

Holiness in person 'driving in prodigious purple state,' dim within the shadows of his coach, like some dusky Hindoo idol in the depths of its shrine.

'I have looked along the grassy vistas of the Appian Way and seen the topmost stone-work of the Coliseum. . . . I've seen the Tiber hurrying along, as swift and dirty as History! I've seen troops of little tonsured neophytes clad in scarlet, marching and countermarching. . . . In fine I've seen Rome!

'*Que vous en dirai-je?*' he cries at the end. 'What can I say to you? At last—for the first time—*I live!*'

IV

A 'PASSIONATE PILGRIM'

IN A typical early story by Henry James, a young American who has voyaged to Italy perorates: I have come on a pilgrimage. To understand what I mean, you must have lived, as I have lived, in a land beyond the seas, barren of romance and grace. This Italy of yours, on whose threshold I stand, is the home of history, of beauty, of art. . . . The notion of a 'pilgrimage,' then, is seldom removed from the thoughts of Henry James for the whole wistful, mobile first half of his life. His was a pathetic Odyssey lasting many years and pursued through divers climates and cities, in quest of the missed and longed-for color, form, antiquity even, such as shaped itself as most desirable for what was at first a rather romantic imagination. Later, as he knew his mind better, the beautiful 'things' became a positive need, the sine qua non and the necessary conditions for creative effort. They symbolized or associated themselves with a form of life filled with leisure, cultivated passions, and finished conversation, that was unthinkable in his poor, provincial States.

It may be opposed that 'the world was too much

with him,' that externals of architecture, language, manners, equipage, consoled him too easily. True, an earlier America had called forth spirits of a different stamp: Emerson, who plodded through frozen mud to address his earnest farmers; and Thoreau, who traveled only within a stone's throw of a frog-pond. These seers had sought only moral rewards rather than sensuous ones; and now, in another day, the conscience of Henry James—fastidious, reticent, continent, to be sure—turned toward a more worldly beauty. He was a 'snob' if you wished—but he was one who would have embraced a navvy who could write a good sentence! Was his art a *decadent* one, as the whole period which he and Howells dominated in American letters, with its aching for gentility, repose, order, has been defined? Certainly, if the development from simplicity and rudeness toward complexity and consciousness is decadent. The ways of genius are never alike. Henry James was never to be a homely poet of the land or of the joys of the simple poor. He was a man primarily of sensibility; he was dyspeptic and even a little neurotic. But his art was to be no less intense or passionate, within its smaller microcosm, than that of the more universal Dickens, the elemental Dostoevski.

And what is most profoundly, most intimately, American—more truly so, surely, than the merely aggressive or muscular qualities expected, for no reason whatsoever, of an American literature—was his permanent condition of yearning and voyaging toward the sanctuaries of the beautiful. No European embarked on such 'passionate pilgrimages'; no Frenchman, no Italian, scanned the national shrines so devotedly. The nostalgia and the need was something deeply American, and far from constituting a backward step, Henry James's example was to be an early and daring forecast of a later state of mind and a later culture. His followers today are many, in Montmartre, Tahiti, or the Bay of Naples. But having so refined upon himself, having become so acutely attentive, inquiring, and sensitive—in the unconscious 'mission' of civilizing his compatriots—he came to appear, as many observed, particularly cultivated and exquisite to the Europeans.

The 'holy places' were not to be found, neither in Italy, nor in France, nor in England; and in his bafflement the exquisite was to become a portentous figure in the end, as much to the Europeans who disabused him as to the Americans. For those who have deprecated his curious earthly wanderings have utterly failed to understand that James's Great Good Place—like Baudelaire's 'Out of the World,' like Rimbaud's *Pays Exotiques*—had no geography whatsoever!

But returning now and again from foreign scenes the American absentee would be stirred by all sorts of curious anticipations. Then, at sight of the white wooden buildings and sordid, littered docks, of the whole familiar, impoverished scene, deep pangs would often arise at the contrasts so forcibly perceived. It was with the feeling of a heavy weight settling upon the heart that the repatriated, one after another, uttered their lament and then subsided into their place on the great unendowed, unentertained continent.

'I agree with you as to the wants one feels at home,' wrote James Russell Lowell to his friend Story on the occasion of his return from Germany. 'When I look back and think how much in me might have earlier and kindlier developed, I feel bitter. . . .' The wants which Lowell perceived were declared by his colleague, Norton, to be in scale only 'with the grandeur of our opportunities. . . . So that one might rejoice to be an American, after all, even while seeing how far we fall short, and how much must be done to make life here what it might be.' And he concludes, '*To be contented here one must work.*'

Even William James, whom we find at all moments so far apart from his brother, gives words upon at least one occasion to such a sadness of home-coming as other nationals would find hard to understand. 'Oh, the thin grass and ragged waysides,' he moans, 'the poverty-stricken land, and sad American sunlight over all—sad because so empty. . . . The coming back makes one feel so strangely sad and hardens one in the resolution never to go away again unless one can go to end one's days. . . . As England struck me newly and differently last time, so America now—force and directness in the people, but a terrible grimness, more ugliness than I ever realized in things, and a greater weakness in nature's beauties, such as it is.

'One must pitch one's whole sensibility in a different key—' he resumes with much good grace and wisdom, 'then gradually the quantum of personal happiness of which one is susceptible fills the cup—but the moment of change of key is lonesome. . . .'

For Henry James there was to be no easy subsidence into the American keynote. He became the victim of unrest; an incessant debate raged within him, and the American years dragged by as a lengthening chain, a torment of losses and regrets. The nostalgic poison had been distilled for him; the future presented to him but as a single intense question: Was he to spend it in brooding exile, or might he somehow come into his 'own'?

Restored to America, his heart fell, and the sense of freedom passed from him as he found himself swimming again in the 'great tepid bath of democracy.' In Europe he could haunt the fountainheads of art as much as he willed, but was it not bitter to become a lonely cosmopolite, a man without a country, who might pass years in talk largely with *garçons de café;* who, loving the Italian language, must pay some one to converse in it with him! In either case, he had great misgivings; and for a long time, floating between two worlds, now in Western Europe, now in Massachusetts—there were five crossings of the gray Atlantic within three years—he oscillated painfully between the native society which repelled him and the exotic one which seemed to reward him so little. His trouble and faltering clouds the correspondence of these years and dominates a great part of his early writings.

Here was Cambridge, little Cambridge, again! Here were the old corners and landmarks, the red brick houses, and best of all the high thin elms, spreading aloft, looped and drooping over the old streets and commons. It was amazing 'how little Cambridge was ever his affair.' What lay before him now? Everything, of course. Since he proposed to be a novelist of manners, of the human comedy, none perceived better than he the magnitude of the task and the risks.

'Naked come we into a naked world,' says one of his early characters. 'There's a certain grandeur in the lack of decoration, a certain heroic strain in that young imagination of ours which finds nothing made to its hands, which has to invent its own traditions and raise high in the morning-air with a ringing hammer and nails, the castles in which we dwell.'

And yet when one cast about for subjects the local material that offered itself was sparse and uniform.

And if one tended to be critical of it, if one wanted to speak freely, among so many female chroniclers, what would one arrive at?

'The face of nature and civilization in this our country,' he commented now with a tempered optimism, 'is to a certain point a very sufficient literary field. But it will only yield its secrets to a really *grasping* imagination. . . . To write well and worthily of American things one needs even more than elsewhere to be a master. But unfortunately one is less. . . .'

The burdens, the dangers, that loomed before the American artist were to be an obsession with him and form the *Leitmotif* of the stories written at this period. *A Madonna of the Future* (1871) is the portrait of one of those unhappy exiles—so obviously conceived from the case of Washington Allston or William Page—whose genius has come to grief, whose masterpiece, never to be completed, turns into a mysterious blank with the passage of the years.

'We're the *disinherited* of art!' cries the wrecked painter. 'We're condemned to be superficial! We're excluded from the magic circle! The soil of American perception is a poor little barren artificial deposit. Yes! we're wedded to imperfection! An American, to excel, has just ten times as much to learn as a European! We lack the deeper sense. We have neither taste nor force. How should we have them? Our crude and garish climate, our silent past, our deafening present, the constant pressure about us of unlovely conditions, are as void of all that nourishes and prompts and inspires the artist as my sad heart is in saying so! We poor aspirants must live in perpetual exile. . . .'

Henry James is by no means convinced at this time that the lot of the uprooted cosmopolitan is an unmixed blessing. He revisits Rome, gathering 'priceless impressions' for *Roderick Hudson*, his most serious attempt thus far at the novel. But the intensity of the youthful experience can scarcely be duplicated. Has the old enchantment of Rome passed? And Florence too has turned into an empty, melancholy, bankrupt place—an old sleeping, soundless city like Pisa. A sadness of decline had touched the permanent colony of Americans, whom he observes with tremendous interest. The relics and fragments of the ancient group which circulated about William Wetmore Story seem pathetically broken down. 'Neither in its meridian nor its decline had it shown any irresistible charm or strength,' he reflects.

The *débâcle* of the emancipated American in the distracting and languefying climate of Rome is a warning to him, and it becomes the major theme of *Roderick Hudson.* There would be the young American sculptor, oddly transplanted from the remotest depths of New England to the Eternal City. He undergoes the 'Europeanizing process' and vows that he will die in the shadow of St. Peter's. A few months of Roman life bring a welter of beautiful sensations and experiences. 'As he looked back on those full-flavored weeks, he drew a long breath of satisfaction, almost of relief.' But soon the fatal eclipse begins; the larger freedom of sense and imagination are more than he can safely bear; he becomes a prey to the gambling passion and the fool of woman. His carvings stand incomplete and abandoned. . . . Plainly Henry James fears the effects of expatriation as much as the compromises of an American career. He himself is as yet subject to homesickness and has all the signs of a divided spirit.

'What is the meaning of this destiny of desolate exile—' he writes from abroad to Howells, 'this dreary necessity of having month after month to do without our friends for the sake of this arrogant old Europe which so little befriends us?'

And at times he felt that he was establishing the merest surface relations only with the world into which he sought to penetrate. You were free to wander down roads everywhere and speculate upon what lovely private gardens were sheltered behind the high walls, what life throbbed behind the drawn persiennes of the great windows. Failing to be initiated into the *mise en scène* of European life, he wondered if he were destined to strike roots nowhere, once having abandoned his native soil!

'Relish Europe as we may, we belong much more to that rather than this,' he wrote to a brilliant Cambridge lady, 'and we stand in a much less factitious and artificial relation to it. I feel forever how Europe keeps holding one at arm's length, and condemning one to a meager scraping of the surface.'

2

It was at this time, in 1873, that William James, ailing in health, came to join his somewhat younger brother in Italy for a vacation. The feeling between the two brothers was unusually warm, but in all other respects they were virtually at opposite poles.

A debate ensued between them which was prolonged for a score of years and is of the utmost interest for us a half-century later. By the sharp contrast of their natures they each arrived at strikingly different solutions of their personal problems.

William, as we have seen, was impulsive, downright, prompt to react, where Henry James was deliberate, slow of speech, brooding or complex. And again William, who resembled in greater degree his remarkable father, had inherited the identical interest in general ideas—although this impulse seems weaker in the end than the other's passion for the absolute in art.

The older brother had but recently recovered from ill health and morbid depressions; emerging, after long struggles with his conscience, from the more painful phase of agnosticism, he had reached a state of mind that was both serene and vigorous. What tranquillized him was that he had decided to abandon philosophy. Having groped so long and suffered so much in the search for a comprehensive view of life, he had concluded that it was useless. 'Philosophy,' he said, 'breeds hypochondria . . . it is a curse.' Philosophy had, in short, never been a consolation and a sanctuary for him; it was rather, as Santayana observed, 'a maze in which he happened to find himself, and what he was looking for was a way out.'

His terror of metaphysics was probably only equaled by his fear and his naïveté about art, as his brother practiced it. He was horrified at the life of leisure and introspection Henry led, which would have thrown him into the blackest confusion or melancholy. That was what he would seek to escape from, and his secret would be hard work and self-oblivion, the hard work that Norton had said an American must have in order to retain his reason. Despite his skepticism about science, there was the method of 'pragmatism' in any case, the principle of judgment developed by the ill-starred Peirce and himself, which enabled one to live precariously upon the eternal, mysterious stream of experience. But deeper than pragmatism was his inheritance from the earlier American background of a moral earnestness or hopefulness that prevailed over his skepticism. Intensely democratic and sharing the passions of liberalism, he was far from cynical in his morals and believed that 'certain thoughts and hopes, those familiar to a liberal Protestantism, were every man's true friends in life.' And so like most Americans, William James felt the call of the future and believed that it could be made far better, totally other, than the past.

Possessing pragmatism, then, and a passion for so much hard work as brought forgetfulness of self, it will be seen that William James was really adjusted to the conditions of American life, and headed even for a certain 'success.' The pioneering in psychology, the interesting school of philosophy founded by him at Harvard, were to bring him wide repute, while the impact of his unconventional and lucid criticism was to be felt by European thought as well. For in terror of his brother's example, his own style became painfully plain and racy, shunning the niceties of language and the tortuous processes of metaphysics which he made no secret of despising. . . .

Europe then was calculated to stir William James but rarely, and then only in certain moods of a sentimental poetry. In Florence, in 1873, we find him grumbling, bantering and disputing with his brother. For his part, as he plodded his way every morning o'er steps of broken thrones and temples, he could derive little joy either from antiquity or the life of art. In his bluff and impulsive way he belabors Henry for his absorption in form to the loss of subject and earnestly he warns him against prolonging his sojourn in the 'lands of happiness and self-oblivion.'

'All this dead civilization, crowding upon one's consciousness,' he observes, 'forces the mind open again, and what my mind wants most is practical tasks.' (It was a presage of the William James who would become a veritable bull-in-the-china-shop for Hegelians!) 'My very enjoyment of what here belongs to the "hoary eld," has done more,' he ruminates, 'to reconcile me to the present hour, business, factories, etc., than anything I ever experienced.' He ended simply by describing himself as a barbarian mind having a 'plain Yankee stomach,' peculiarly immune to history and unable to endure either French or Roman ways of being and doing things, one who could never, in short, call Rome 'my country' or 'city of my soul,' like the too *literary* Henry.

It may be seen, then, how soundly patriotic were William James's reactions to the deep, rich old world; and there is little doubt that Henry, who needed only such admonitions to harden him, resorted often to caricaturing his brother's views quite recognizably in the tales which he was writing. But there are also times when William James strikes a higher and braver note in the vivacious debates with his brother and presents the other side of the issue powerfully enough.

'Europe,' he would plead, 'has been made what it is by men staying in their homes and fighting stubbornly generation after generation for all the beauty, comfort, order that they have got—we must abide and do the same. . . . A man always pays in one way or another for expatriation, for detachment from his plain, primary heritage.'

And in the years that followed, William persisted earnestly in the effort to bring his brother back. Would he return for good, he wrote him from Cambridge in 1874, or would he fix himself permanently in Europe? He must make his choice; everything hung upon it. He must come now and establish his roots in America, before it was too late!

'I shall go,' Henry replies from Florence, 'with the full provision that I shall not find life at home *simpatico,* but rather painfully and, as regards literary work, the reverse. But I shrink from Willy's apparent assumption that going now is to pledge myself to stay forever. I feel as if my three years in Europe (with much of them so *maladif*) were a very moderate allowance . . . and I don't think I could really hold my head up if I didn't hope to eat a bigger slice of the pudding. . . .'

The business of touring plays an enormous part in the writings of Henry James's first manner.

Nearly all the characters in *The Pension Beaurepas*, *Roderick Hudson*, *The Point of View*, *The International Episode*, *Four Meetings*, *Daisy Miller*, *The American*, and many others, go touring toward the more glamorous eastern continent. These are stories of ideas rather than of the passions, as a rule; the moral customs, the methods of pleasure, of hunting a mate, as among the Yankees, are contrasted with the art of living of Europeans, often with great impartiality and most often to the clear discredit of the Yankees. Thus it is little wonder that the success of the International Tales was so slight, for in addition to being frankly critical of the national folk-ways in their tone, they were—if a little pallid and stilted at moments—more imaginative, wittier, worldlier, and more gracefully written than any prose fiction that appeared in America between 1870 and 1880.

The Americans he pictures move fatally from simplicity to complexity. It is as if, having passed through preliminary hardships and trials, having acquired the means for life, they now reach out toward the amenities of it. Thus they go 'gathering up a little European culture,' and emboldened, they sometimes storm the very citadels of civilization. Now it is an American doctor who tries to marry a lovely pedigreed English beauty in the face of her whole fox-hunting clan, as in the story *Lady Barberina*. A King of Bathtubs, properly named Newman, leaves the scenes of his triumphs in Wall Street and courts a noble French lady, involving himself deeply in an old-world atmosphere of mysticism and tragedy, finding, in fact, a chasm between two worlds and two races so broad that all his indomitable energy, self-confidence, and business ingenuity cannot quite manage it.

The whole motive of the International Tales, then, was to offer his innocent compatriots a view of a more complex and conscious world, so that by the variety of types and classes, and heritage, and all those graces and refinements of leisure and conversations in gardens, a brave demonstration might be made against the mere brassy 'show of existence' which passed for life in America.

He had taken his stand; he was for 'civilization,' the continuous process of which was exemplified in the prolonged and still vital Renaissance, whose symbols he saluted so passionately in Italy or France or England—he was for this against that which he deemed barbarism, all that great materialistic intensity with which the masses of his compatriots had been infected. For in America no one *lived* in the true, the freer and larger, sense. And from beginning to end Henry James's writings were a plea for freedom, for the right to live, in one's own light, as full a life as possible.

The very novel which he had completed in 1874—and then appearing with so little result in the *Atlantic*—was such a plea for freedom. 'When you expect a man to produce beautiful and wonderful works of art,' he has Roderick Hudson say, 'you ought to allow him a certain freedom of action, you ought to give him a long rope, you ought to let him follow his fancy wherever he thinks he may find it! You demand of us to be imaginative, and yet you deny us that which feeds the imagination! In labor we must be as passionate as the inspired sybil; in life mere machines. It won't do. . . .'

The poignant drama of the young cosmopolitan, who had absorbed 'the virus of Europe,' whose preferences were clearly as yet romantic, was evoked always anew for him by the episode of repatriation. Would he submit to the great leveling power of the country, with its imposed restrictions of taste and opinion? Would he become a part of the fixed and bare landscape—like Howells? Would he be writing another and still another little New England tale for the *Atlantic*, while the shallow tides of a provincial life—'all thin and diluted'—closed over his sad head?

And so the young returned absentee of James's earlier fictions (such as *The Point of View*) finds himself consumed with the love of the farther shore. He doesn't get on at all! He has simply dropped out of his place; and now he is a stranger here who finds it hard to believe that he ever was a native.

'It's very hard, very cold, very vacant. I think of your warm rich Paris; I think of the Boulevard

Saint Michel on the mild spring evenings. . . . The sense there is of a supreme splendor and an incomparable arrangement, yet there is a kind of tone, of body, in the radiance; the mighty murmur of the ripest civilization in the world comes in; the dear old *peuple de Paris,* the most interesting people in the world, pass by. . . .'

The outcry mounts to a tone of hysteria as our young man tosses miserably in his hotel bed at night, unable to sleep for all the strange inhuman sounds that assail him: 'I toss and groan. I spring up to call for some help, some remedy. But there's no bell and I feel desolate and weak. There's only a strange orifice in the wall, through which the traveler in distress may transmit his appeal. I fill it with incoherent sounds, and sounds more incoherent come back to me. A hollow, impersonal voice wishes to know what I want, and the very question paralyzes me. I want everything—I want my little corner of Paris; *I want the rich, the deep, the dark old world. I want to be out of this horrible* place. . . .'

Henry James embarked again in 1875, resolved to live forever in Europe.

3

He was in Paris again—'glittering, charming, civilized Paris!' For a time he truly believed that he might grow into an old and contented Parisian; he felt himself likely to strike roots into the Parisian soil and let them grow tangled and tenacious there. The great merit of the place, as he confided to Howells—who envied him, and whom he urged in vain to come—was that one was free, one could arrange one's life absolutely as one pleased; there were facilities for every kind of habit and taste, and '*everything was understood and accepted.*' Paris itself was meanwhile a sort of painted backdrop, shifting and changing, but always there to be looked at when you pleased, or to be comfortably ignored.

He haunted the hallowed Théâtre Français and soon learned by heart its whole repertory of Scribe, Dumas *fils*, Sardou. He had even been introduced a little behind the scenes. . . .

He circulated also in certain salons of the Faubourg Saint Germain, becoming 'gorged with music' at Mme. de Bloqueville's and even at Mme. Viardot's. One perceived instantly the more curious and free relationships which flourished in the easier Parisian soil. A gay, athletic, rosy-cheeked young man named Maupassant told him thick tales of innumerable conquests of society women. And if the Europeans seemed a little 'corrupt' by New England standards, they knew how to entertain themselves with a spontaneity that Americans sadly lacked. 'It was both strange and sweet to see poor Turgenev acting charades of the most extravagant description, dressed out in old shawls and masks, going on all fours, etc.

Fancy Americans like Longfellow, Lowell, or Charles Norton doing the like, and every Sunday evening!'

What was most fortunate of all, however, was that he had penetrated, thanks to his remarkable sense of the language, into the literary fraternity of Paris. And more, he had been admitted into the most vital, the most emancipated, literary group in the world: the circle of Gustave Flaubert, the realistic 'sons of Balzac,' who numbered among them, besides the incomparable author of *Madame Bovary*, Goncourt, Zola, Daudet, the youthful Maupassant, and the great Russian, Turgenev. Almost alone among those who wrote English, Henry James, all attention, all conscious of his good luck, absorbed and transmitted the ideas of the new French masters of the novel, who stood 'so far away from our Anglo-Saxon Protestant, moralistic, conventional standards . . . and judged things with a freedom and spontaneity in which I found a perpetual refreshment.'

Flaubert was a rotund giant, with a receding mane of blond hair, great drooping yellow mustaches, and the rosy cheeks and pale blue eyes of a child. On Sundays, in the little white and gold drawing-room of the rue Murillo, among his twenty or thirty visitors who all stood drinking or smoking, he held forth, he 'bellowed.' Or now the elegant Edmond de Goncourt, of the young face and white hair, or the handsome Daudet, or the pale but immensely 'honest' Zola took part in the passionate discussion of their effort and experiment, or exchanged free confidences on their current work, on their plans and ambitions. For James it was impressive in the highest degree, since he had never been privileged to see artistic conviction, artistic passion, so systematic and so articulate.

Thus Flaubert, to the great amusement of his company, would tell of his researches for *Buvard et Pécuchet*, in which he made a vast compendium of the commonplace utterance, the imbecilities, of the *petit bourgeois*. Or Zola, who was writing a book of the common people (*L'Assommoir*), would announce that he was making a dictionary of 'all the bad words of the language, those with which the speech of the workingman bristles. . . .' He announced this without bravado and without apology, simply as an interesting idea that had come to him.

All of them, the young American novelist felt, were laboring, 'with a truly infernal intelligence of art, form, manner' toward character, toward particular truth. How deliberately, how patiently, they went about planning and building their effects! They were architects of prose. James heard for the first time Zola's plan of the twenty-volume Rougon-Macquart cycle. ('The pyramid was planned and the site staked by the young builder.') The lesson of discipline was stamped upon his mind. It figured in the example of the anchoretic Flaubert, who labored so desperately, so pathetically, over his pages, who held that 'nothing comes of itself,' that only by fasting and prayer and pursuit, by long waits and watches, were the great effects gained; or in that of Zola, who with such scanty equipment set forth resolutely on his colossal schemes.

What fine dressings he heard them give the Philistines—for even in France there were such—and he perceived that the great conviction that held them together was that art and morality were two separate things. Everything else was to be secondary to their 'studies from life'; the principle of exact, painstaking, unshrinking observation was paramount for the Naturalists. Like them, Henry James learned to take notes of everything he saw or heard, and in the enthusiasm of his discoveries, he felt more and more pleased at his distance from the narrow house of New England letters.

It was Turgenev, however, from whom he drew the most interesting and fruitful impressions. He was one of the great Europeans, and his gift, he felt, was that of being essentially impersonal, objective, about the human type. Tall, white-haired, with the aristocratic bearing of the great landowner that he was, Henry James found him utterly 'adorable' in conversation, and without a particle of vanity, or that eagerness of self-reference which so often accompanies great reputations. Turgenev was a cosmopolite and an émigré by force of circumstances. He too had felt his own people rude and uncultivated; his native

Russian society was his despair, and his own land lay sunken in ignorance, crushed under the weight of feudal and barbarous institutions.

It is almost impossible to miss the powerful suggestions which Turgenev's example threw off. He was at odds with Russia; he had been compelled by his larger personal needs to seek the richer, more responsive western European scene, and to live thus in exile, as it were, for the greater part of his life; so that his compatriots deemed him French. For European civilization sat lightly as yet upon immense, semi-Asiatic Russia, and minds were divided then, as now, as to which influence should rule her. In the capitals of Europe, at the universities, one met as many Russian tourists in pursuit of 'culture' in 1875, as Americans in 1930.

Turgenev was for Europe rather than for orthodox or Holy Russia. The great drama of his life, as James saw it then, was the struggle for a better state of things in his country. Whatever his physical separation, he had his 'mission,' his part to play among his distant countrymen. He clung always to his Russian characters, whether placed in the native milieu or abroad under the 'Europeanizing process.' And did not the biting satire of his prose rouse them, lash them to consciousness? (It was a cardinal principle of realism that one must know one's ground, one must write only of that which one knew, that with which one was saturated. And so Turgenev returned every summer to his estate in the interior of Russia, steeping himself again in the deep feelings, the memories of early years, the richness of the native tongue, and the wide Russian horizons.)

The influence and example of Turgenev worked profoundly upon the young novelist. The novels of James's 'middle years' were to be objective, ironical, realistic. They were simply and expertly organized, for he acquired a horror for the unwieldy, interminable, 'three-decker' chronicles of Victorian England. At their best, as in *Daisy Miller*, *An International Episode*, *The Portrait of a Lady*, they exhibited economy, suppressed the inessential, and left the play of satire and drama 'suggestive' and implicit in a degree that was unheard of as yet in the plain-spoken, quasi-humorous, and pedestrian Anglo-Saxon prose. At an extremely dark period, Henry James carried over into the English language—and it was by no means easy—the more lucent and pointed qualities, the precise structural form, of French and Russian fiction. At extremes, moreover, as in the case of the excessively realistic *Washington Square* and the even more perversely faithful *Bostonians*, he sought diligently for the atmosphere of place, and he submitted his art to characters of the most rigidly limited and neutral type. And unobtrusively, too unobtrusively playing, one thinks, his irony made appeal for a 'better state of things' among his distant Bostonians and New Yorkers. His irony, as Howells said, was of the kind that 'does not blink at our foibles.' So that, after many years of European life, James still said: 'I have always my eyes on my native land. . . .' Like Turgenev, he restricted himself to the characters and the situations which he clearly and deeply knew; he clung to American character, but placed it more and more frequently upon the narrow and shifting ground of the international scene, where the tourist or exile among strange, uprooted coteries passes his obscure, provisory, and parasite existence. But here the parallel with Turgenev ends, since the one would draw deeply and satisfyingly upon the race-character, the age-old traditions of his impassioned countrymen, while the other searched and grasped vainly for such points of departure, for constants, values, or landmarks, as were simply obliterated in the eternal flux of dynamic America.

4

Paris was to be but a stage in the long pilgrimage. James turned against Paris in weariness and satiety, while the French mind and its utterance fell from him like an outworn garment.

He left the literary fraternity of Flaubert and Zola without regrets, and with a veritable bitterness. He had felt himself alien, despite his laboriously perfect French. He had made no permanent relations. There were fifty reasons why he could not become intimate with them; he didn't like their wares, and they didn't like any others. And besides, they weren't really inviting at bottom.

In the Parisian air, which is so widely granted to be cosmopolitan, the great Frenchmen become deeply, inscrutably provincial. They give little ear to what is done, to what goes on, elsewhere. Turgenev had marked this and suffered from it. And James said to his friend Edmund Gosse, 'They never read a line of me. They never even persuaded themselves that there was a line of me which any one could read.' And how should they, Edmund Gosse observes; how should the charming, self-sufficing fellows know what or whether some Barbarian had remotely written? What did they know, for instance, of George Eliot, whose *Daniel Deronda* had appeared at the time of their prolonged discussions of Daudet's lachrymose *Jack!* Henry James's rôle was passive among them. When he had ventured to belittle Prosper Mérimée before Flaubert, the master had turned upon him furiously, abusing him unmercifully, bellowing that he knew nothing whatsoever of style. One recalls that Zola also had been roundly rated on the same score. But the American novelist had been deeply disturbed; even if one ignores his strong and candid vanity, the incident had reinforced his sense of foreignness, of a want of kinship with these men. And then, he had misgivings of his own. The indefatigable William wrote him from Cambridge that he was losing his hold upon the language, that his letters bristled with Gallicisms; and one feels that this is something that may have pricked him as strongly as any other consideration.

And so during a summer's stay at the lovely Channel resort of Etretat, he began to look with rising curiosity at the frequently visible English shore.

'I have done with 'em forever,' he wrote to Willy, 'and am turning English all over. I desire only to feed on English life and the contact of English minds.'

He was reduced to a good deal of boulevard and third-rate Americanism. Ah! if he had but a single good friend in London!

The expatriate finds himself as a rule isolated; his friendships are transient, his social position equivocal. And if one suffers indignities, if one becomes bored at sheer ugliness and dreariness, one is prone to flight again, unable to determine whether it is universal, distressing human nature or the specific country of his residence that provides the disturbing factor.

In England, in 'poor, smutty,. dusky, Philistine London,' James soon began to feel most at home. He had seen and talked with a considerable number of people, but he had become familiar, as he confesses, with almost none.

'I find myself a great deal more of a cosmopolitan (thanks to that combination of the continent and the U.S.A., which has formed my lot) and to be a cosmopolitan—to have become by force of circumstances a cosmopolitan—is to be a good deal alone.'

There was so much in English life and English character that offered itself irresistibly as pin-cushions to criticism and irony. There were times when the fog, the smoke, the universal uncleanliness, the combined unwieldiness and flatness, overwhelmed his spirit and made him lose all patience with the English, fifteen times a day—but in the end, despite the clearest sense of their deficits and an enduring tendency to take wing for Italy and Paris, he clung to them, finding them 'more largely nourished, deeper, denser, stronger, more complete than other folk.'

The period could scarcely have been more stimulating anywhere. It was the time of Disraeli and Gladstone, and the final precarious thrust of Imperial expansion in a world that was alive with enemies. It was still the broad noon hour of Victorian culture and policy, while echoes of an older English society, with its ingrained love of violence in its amusements or sports, still prevailed. It was a day of amazing prosperity and activity; an elaborate, intricate old ruling-class cleaved bitterly to its spoils and its ancient ways while social dangers, a hundredfold intensified, lurked on every side. After the small-town life of New York and Boston, the spectacle of immense London was calculated to delight this lover of world-cities.

And besides, they had received him; they had been inviting as the English seldom are. He had wanted people, he had wanted above all 'a *régal* of intelligent and suggestive society'; and he found it. He went 'everywhere,' sedately, graciously, watchfully, though never prominently, this haunter of British society, this impassioned student of London life. His air was as yet a little formal and frightened at thirty or thirty-five, as Gosse tells us. There was something shadowy about his face, framed in dark brown hair, cut short in the Paris fashion, and in his equally dark beard. He was far from the impressive presence, benign, urbane, with the manner of a stout and worldly prelate, which he later became and which Sargent caught in the clever portrait. But he frankly desired entrance into English society; he desired to 'be taken seriously,' holding that the pursuit of a social success was a legitimate object. If one regarded 'life as an art,' then it were most profitable to approach that portion of human society which represented the consummation of the energies and efforts of an age. He avoided thus, he thought, the merely instrumental or purposeless, by taking the more perfect human types. 'The idle and the rich of society,' he said one day to the French painter, Jacques Emile Blanche, 'have more time to occupy themselves with one another, to cultivate their passions, which are less rudimentary, in general, than those of other humans, who must provide hour after hour for their own living, far removed from those influences which form *civilization*, the beauty of manners. This latter is not indispensable, but it is a patrimony that it would be foolhardy to reject. . . .'

In his choice of grounds upon which he was to study life, to listen endlessly, to take notes, to saturate himself, James was curiously the prototype of Marcel Proust, and for much the same aesthetic reasons.

His success (perhaps owing to the wing of the friendly ambassador, Mr. Lowell) is astonishing. He moves in the full rout of Mayfair, during the 'season.' He breakfasts with Lord Houghton, who knows 'every one' and takes him everywhere dotingly. He lunches with Tennyson (so 'different from one's conception of him'), whom he finds swarthy and scraggy, with a rustic accent and much talk of port and tobacco, seeming altogether 'like a creature of some primordial English stock, a thousand miles away from American manufacture.' He dines also with Mr. Gladstone, whose conversation has an ease, a flawless abandon, and yet an extreme urbanity—plainly a man of genius. And there is the amazing Swinburne, to whom he grants his frightened admiration, the 'thundering' Spencer, the young-looking John Morley, who is silent, but who has done much. And there are women, like Mrs. Fanny Kemble, who, finding Mr. James so admirable a listener, pour out a thousand and one tales of Mayfair nights which ravish the hunter of ironies, of nuances and disillusionment.

'When they have made their money,' an American diplomat wrote of the English, to his President, 'they cultivate their minds and their gardens and entertain their friends.' And it was true, if one penetrated to this side of the race which stole continents unctuously and believed that the earth belonged to it, there was impressive evidence of the success of their form of life. The retired officer, twenty-five miles out of London, had his house that was five hundred years old, his ten acres of garden, his immense lawn, his trees; and he walked you all over this, he sat out of doors and served you tea, he took life rationally, he exhibited the best manners in the world, he talked. . . . Nothing was ever abolished in England; nothing was ever changed. The pot-herbs on judges' desks dated from Defoe's time, and even further back the Horse Guards, the liveried attendants of the Bank of England, the great tea-parties when the rhododendrons bloomed.

Henry James, living in the midst of this preferred 'material,' submitted himself without reserve to 'the Londonizing process.' One has a glimpse of him in 1880 at Mentmore, the Scottish country-seat of Lord Rosebery, who wore his youth, his literary talent, his cleverness, his immense fortune (thanks to a Rothschild wife) with rare tact and bonhomie. The house is a huge modern palace filled with wonderful objects of art collected by Lady Rosebery's father. Tea is served in a great glittering hall. There is shooting and riding to the hounds, and a costume ball in the evening, at which the famous beauty, Mrs. Langtry, dances a Highland reel.

Everywhere, Henry James has simply been living up to a standard—'my charming little standard . . . of wit, of grace, of good manners, of vivacity, of urbanity, of intelligence, of what marks an easy and natural style of intercourse . . .' and he has become a good enough Englishman to relish his personal independence, 'to respect inveterately my own habits, and do, wherever I may be, only exactly what I want.' For within the limits of that discretion and provided that one grasped the spirit of conventions which the English are famed for, one could do everything. Like Lambert Strether in *The Ambassadors*, he welcomed living with all his senses; he looked about him a great deal, and enjoyed and sniffed. It was not as if he drank himself to death, or ran after too many women!

It has been remarked that the kind of life, in Europe and in England, which might have been thought too trifling to bear the weight of a powerful scrutiny, was exactly the life that Henry James pursued. He accorded the 'great world' a deference it is little accustomed to receiving, and in this world —one suspects it was often quite dull and middle-class—he moved about with a certain elegance and discretion, living up to his 'standard'—his charming little standard. But when we recall how corrupt and brutal under the surface this very society appeared to Englishmen—and that James himself was to end by perceiving this—we can only explain his predilection for such a London life as a recoil from the crudeness of American social character.

His mode of life is unmistakably patterned after the idealized theory of a wistful American who believes that the European and chiefly the British upper class has reached a gentler perfection in the art of living. Leisure is gracefully employed here; wealth has embellished itself, as nowhere in the United States. To pass one's time in much conversation, to keep to a rather amateur, 'purist' attitude toward his art—rather than a business attitude such as would alone have been tolerated in the States—was unthinkable in an American. There only the semblance of hard work passed for virtue; its automatism alone brought relief from a thousand aches, misgivings, disillusionments. The finger of derision would have been pointed by every one at the apparently idle, the merely gallantly employed, young man. And so the more Henry James grew inured to and enjoyed his London life, found himself making happy progress with his work, the more American life came to seem incredible, on the whole. The tone of his books at this period, *Daisy Miller*, *The Europeans*, *The Life of Hawthorne*, *The Bostonians*, distinctly reflects his various heresies; alarm and indignation mounted in the reading circles of Boston.

A spirited controversy arose over the biography of Hawthorne which James contributed to Morley's series of English Men of Letters, in 1879. Henry James had pointed out coldly the lesson of 'provincialism,' to whose fatal effects he had ascribed the partial failure of the author of *The Scarlet Letter*. 'It takes an old civilization to set a novelist in motion,' he wrote. 'It is on manners, customs, usages, habits, forms, upon all these things matured and established, that a novelist lives—they are the very stuff his work is made of.'

Howells had replied, though without asperity, that it was well, after all, that there was 'no sovereign, no court, no aristocracy, no clergy, no church, no country gentlemen, palaces, nor manor houses'—since in the absence of such dreary and worn-out paraphernalia, 'we have simply the whole of human life left.'

Other impetuous patriots, of the type of Colonel Thomas Wentworth Higginson, had taken up the cudgels more briskly. 'He does not quite appreciate the strong point of republicanism. . . .' Mr. James desired perhaps a monarchical society for the United States? It is highly doubtful, however, that this was the novelist's object. All his political notions, when he had them, were liberal, in accordance with his radical background and friendships. But there was clearly a disparity between his artistic inventiveness and his moral principles. He was instinctively, profoundly conservative, because he was for civilization, and civilization had become conditioned for him by certain tactile and visual objects and forms, certain virtues and traditions which, vaguely and without historical perspective, he would have liked to preserve. These 'manners, usages, forms,' which composed the cultural heritage of western Europe, he certainly felt counted for little in his own country. In the ruling state of flux and constant eruption, with its undermining and overturning of all social and human values, America suggested to him the picture of civilization at one of its lowest ebbs. The quarrel with America was kept alive by James's subsequent work. A sensation was aroused now by the appearance of *Daisy Miller*, the deft, light-as-air, sentimental study of the American flapper abroad, which became an international success. But it was with *The Bostonians*, some years later in 1886, that James effectively alienated the greatest portion of his public. This work pictured the passing of New England's heroic age of 'plain living and high thinking,' with its decline to quack lectures, fanatical woman evangelists, radicals, mesmerists. Verena Tarrant, the lovely lecturer, is put to use by the Boston feminists; out of her trances much capital, in the way of propaganda, is made in the warfare against 'male tyranny.' Verena is hemmed in, suppressed, her instincts diverted; and her drama is the struggle of love against the rule of the crusading spinsters. As Mr. Van Wyck Brooks has observed, 'It is the picture of a world which seems to consist of nothing but hands, manipulating, repressing, probing, pushing, pulling, exploiting hands.' It is the world, in short, from which Henry James escaped in sacred terror of his own individuality.

There are, moreover, pointed episodes in this book which continue the author's sustained pleading against a benighted provincialism. Thus Verena, arriving by chance in another, a less narrow and militant milieu, where bibelots and objects of art are assembled, where music is played, feels herself wooed and hypnotized for the moment. 'Civilization under such an influence appeared to have done its work . . . life ceased to be a battle. How nice it would be to do that always, not to have so many questions, to sit there on an old Spanish leather chair, with the curtains drawn, keeping out the cold, the darkness, all the big, terrible, cruel world—sit there and listen forever to Schubert and Mendelssohn!'

In nearly all his books Henry James presented men and women of leisure who regarded life as a fine art. There is page after page of conversation, repartee, lecture, much of it brilliant and delicate, which recalls the classical era of Congreve and Pope, despite the accent of Puritan reservation. In *The Europeans*, Mr. Brand, listening to a distinguished foreign pair who visit the depths of New England, exclaims: 'Now I suppose that is what is called conversation, real conversation. It is quite the style we have heard of—the style of Madame de Staël, of Madame Récamier.' And in *The Portrait of a Lady* the conversation of Gilbert Osmond and Mrs. Merle fills Isabel with amazement: 'They talked extremely well; it struck her almost as a dramatic entertainment, rehearsed in advance.' The self-exiled artist urged everywhere, though indirectly, the values he cherished, the civilizing influences; but as we have seen, he succeeded only in arousing incredulity and resentment among his American public. And so the novelist looked with greater hope toward the English, who had after all welcomed him beautifully, whose great literary reviews had opened their doors to him, and among whom a small, faithful public savored his prose, 'of an almost Latin perfection,' and his experiments in form.

'He could never forget that he had somehow to make up to himself for arriving from a totally different social climate,' says his friend, Mr. Percy Lubbock. 'For his own satisfaction he had to wake and toil while others slept.' He could justify his expatriation only by working his life completely into the texture of his new surroundings. It would be useless for him to live where the human drama attracted him most, unless he could grasp it with an assured hand.

'He clung to civilization,' Mr. Lubbock resumes. '*He was faithful throughout to a few yards of town-pavement.*'

After some years he writes to Howells that it is clear that he must 'do,' or half do, England in fiction. . . . 'It has been growing distincter that America fades for me, and as she never trusted me at best, I can trust *her* for effect, no longer.'

Toward 1880, his *Daisy Miller* had been an extraordinary hit in England, and now, applauded, invited everywhere, Henry James knew what it was to be a famous author in London. Gosse, who visited him in his quarters in Bolton Street near Piccadilly, found him stretched on the sofa during the afternoon, unable to rise to greet him. A muscular weakness of his spine, James apologized, obliged him to assume the horizontal position for some hours every day, in order to bear the almost unbroken routine of evening engagements. For he lived in the public eye now; he swam in the glittering confusion of dinner parties.

He referred to himself, nowadays, not without humor, as a *Cockney convaincu.*

'I don't suppose you will envy me for having dined out one hundred and seven times,' he writes at the end of this amazing season to a friend in New England. 'You will simply wonder what can have induced me to perpetrate such a folly, and how I have survived to tell the tale!'

5

There are cycles in a life of society. The remarkable bachelor had desired to be saturated, and had chosen his form of saturation. 'One can mingle in the world with fresh perceptions only when one is young,' he told his brother; and he had taken on board during his Mayfair period such a huge amount of human and social information that he believed he knew the working of English character, at least the mind, 'as well as if he had invented it.'

But such knowledge, worldly knowledge, breeds regret. James was to know evil days, steeped in deception and loneliness. He would react against many long years of London and leave with the sense that all his relations had ended in smoke.

For in a peculiar sense Henry James became a homeless man. There were times when he felt too severely the obtuseness or the suspicion of some elements among the insular people. Certain works which provided studies in the deliberately bad manners of their upper class were scarcely relished, and he noted that his British entertainers found it an entirely new sensation to be 'delicately ironized or satirized' from the American point of view, their conception of the normal in such a relation being that the satire should be all on their side against the Americans. And when a certain English indifference was combined with persistent unpopularity in America, one's situation often looked highly precarious.

From the other side of the Atlantic, the ever-watchful Colonel Higginson, among others, returned to the attack.

'Mr. James's life has been so far transatlantic,' he announced at one time, 'that one hardly knows whether he wishes to be accounted as an American writer.' In those days it was inconceivable that an American might prefer to absent himself from his native land; and to many Americans he was a traitor, a 'backslider,' who had forfeited his birthright.

Henry James's books, which were so generally admired, were often overlooked in discussions of either English or American literature during his lifetime. In the world of letters, as Gosse observed, he endured the singular fate of being a man without a country.

He was aware of the anomaly and bravely made capital of it. 'I aspire to write in such a way that it would be impossible for an outsider to say whether I am at any given moment an American writing about England or an Englishman writing about America . . . and so far from being ashamed of such an ambiguity, I should be exceedingly proud of it, for it would be highly civilized.'

He penetrated far into the arcana of European mummeries and forms and mysteries, only to find, in the end, 'the universal human heart with its greeds, its materialisms, and its Armageddon of passionate disillusionment.' The art of life may have figured to him for a time as a supreme tea-party of a splendid aloofness and beauty. But it was his tragedy, a friend of his observed, 'that no such five o'clock ever sounded for him on the timepieces of the world.'

He was to take thereafter a serene flight toward an art that was wholly absorbed in its own ends. No instance exists of such complete self-immolation in 'art for art's sake.' He had become a great cosmopolitan of literature for whom races, societies, were secondary to his interest in artistic 'difficulty.' He had become an anchorite for whom sex had been destroyed in the interest of style.

V

THOSE WHO STAYED

THERE are phrases which contain the total hope, the popular will, of an age. The slogan 'manifest destiny' resounds through various decades of American history, but louder than ever it rings to us as the major theme of the frenzied expansion years following the Civil War. Not only were rebellious sections overrun and terrorized in the name of manifest destiny; it was as if the whole mass of men, from the lowest immigrant to the great privateer of capital, were galvanized into movement toward the sources of wealth. Those who had known only hunger and cold, those who owned nothing but their two hands, flung themselves with an impassioned unison upon their beckoning fortune.

The social scene—if we glance again at the wonderful situation which a few perverse souls were abandoning for the sake of the European oracle—took on the character more and more of its ruling economic delirium, so that Americans apparently reverted to the Stone Age. The face of the *new man* now appeared definitely; he was certainly 'stripped of all culture'; he moved about without fear of God, without compassions, restraints, responsibilities, with absolutely no such concern for a moral or aesthetic order as still played at least upon the mellower surface of the European societies.

Indeed it was scarcely conceivable that men could be withheld by restraints, stoical or chivalrous, in face of the unheard-of opportunities, the mirages, that appealed on every hand. There was little enough division of sentiment on this score among the masses: men from every walk of life lived in the fever of the gold or land boom, ministers abandoned the Gospel, and army officers threw away the sword. If there were class differences, such as the dissensions of labor and capital, they terminated soon in a solidarity which has never ceased to perplex the academic mind.

It must be remembered that in 1860 the federal government owned in favor of its citizenry of free farmers and artisans (then eighty-five per cent farmers) half the present area of the United States, or one billion acres of land, with all its fabulous subsoil. The imagination falters, then, at the geometrical immensity of the wealth which a benevolent government handed over, in a hurried partition, for nominal sums or by cession, to its political friends and even to the astute first comers. This treasure of coal and oil, of copper and gold and iron and grains, was the spoils of a colossal empire that dropped into the lap of the new pioneers and the new masters. At the same time armies were regimented of disoriented natives and immigrants (in themselves a factor of enormous productive power), who asked only to be led to their promised lands.

The history of the prodigious times, as modern thinkers vision it, should properly ignore the record of senators and presidents. It is the contemporary 'cavemen,' the *condottieri* of oil or steel or railroads, who actually provide an historical pageant no less animated than that of feudalism; *but for obvious reasons these mighty captains have preferred to leave their record inscrutable*, and the chronicle untold of their immensely constructive deeds, by which so many millions of beings were to be uplifted to a superior scale of living and endowed with the luxury of immaculate bath-tubs and horseless carriages.[1]

The whole eye-filling picture must always have stood before the minds of our pathetic 'martyrs of culture' and exiles-for-art; and it is only by keeping it well in view that we can understand their griefs and their bewilderment. The scenes at the nation's capital, during this time, must have brought to the edge of despair all those whose characters had been formed under the gentler ante-bellum order. An *opéra bouffe* ministry sat enthroned under the mili-

[1] 'There were principalities of iron, of copper, of oil, of gold and silver, of timber, of meat,—and soon a great prince arose in each one of these zones of exploitation. The peerage of the new industrial age was: Jay Cooke and Morgan, bankers; William A. Clark, mines; Armour, beef; Hill and Harriman, railroads; Rockefeller, oil; Carnegie, steel. Of these only Morgan had received an education. . . .'—M. and C. A. Beard, *Rise of American Civilization*, New York, 1927.

tary hero in the small political encampment of Washington, palpably dividing the spoils. It was both rural and primitive; in those days there were no theaters, restaurants, no *monde*, no *demi-monde*, no drives, no splendor. And in New York, the cavemen sat everywhere, with clubs, literally, in their hands.

The new rich were curbed in no way by surviving members of an older order in matters of taste or customs. Unchecked by traditions and undisciplined by generations of leisure, these latter-day barons ransacked the palaces and abbeys of mediaeval Europe for their pottery, rugs, mugs, paintings, and the armor of feudal knights. They held great spectacles for their caste amid surroundings which were the replica of Versailles or Sans Souci; there were the dinners of gourmands consumed on horseback, the costume balls at which a Belmont appeared in armor of gold, while chorus girls having the buxom proportions then in fashion popped out of pies or simulated human goldfish in pools. And there were also splendid tableaux of land projects in the west, of gold strikes, of sinister, abortive labor war in Pittsburgh, Cleveland, or Chicago; there were interludes of financial panic, mob movements, riots; there were superb disasters, massacres, and inundations, or fires, devastating whole cities; and there were periodic, picturesque insurrections, when armies of indigents in motley rags slept under the stars and came riding in freight cars from everywhere, came marching, marching behind 'General' Coxie toward Washington—toward bread, gold, the millennium! . . .

In the early 1880s Henry James had made a short visit to the United States (on the occasion of the death of his mother), and we learn from newly disclosed documents that he had passed a short time in Washington and planned a great journey throughout the United States for the sake of learning something about the unimaginable life of the vast hinterland. Picturesque as the period seems in retrospect and exciting as the adventure promised to be, James may have felt premonitions of failure. He may have foreseen the misery and desolation of the actual landscape, the monotony of the great interior plains (after Tuscany and Sussex), and so put off the interesting scheme with little hope of ever resuming it. It was his gifted friend, however, Viscount Bryce, who really embarked at this time on a tour of discovery through the United States; so that we have in his *The American Commonwealth* the valuable reactions of a sensitive foreigner who has examined with a rare detachment all the native forms of life, customs, vices.

Filled with a sense of the future greatness, the immeasurable latent power, of the republic, the young British diplomat wandered and looked pertinaciously everywhere on his long, hard journey. He saw a black, scarred belt of coal and steel stretching from Philadelphia through Pittsburgh and the

Ohio towns to Chicago. It was a replica of Manchester, upon a bigger scale; the jerry-built streets and factories, the blast furnaces and oil derricks, spread themselves darkly everywhere. And throughout the farm lands of the Mississippi valley there was always the same flat country, over which one could not see far because so little raised above it, the same fields and crops, the same rough wooden fences, the same thickets along the stream-edges, the same solitary farm-houses and straggling wood-built villages.

The uniformity of the cities was equally appalling —everywhere the same wide streets, in gridiron arrangement, the same shops, the same Chinese laundries, ice-cream stores, the same large hotels with seedy men hovering about the cheerless entrance halls. In these cities, devoid of anything which bespeaks the past, the foreigner felt his heart sink at the feeling 'that nothing historically interesting ever has happened here, perhaps ever will happen.'

In the far west one might see, as well, the movable mining towns which were defined as 'Hell-on-Wheels,' with their armies of cooks, sutlers, harpies, and gamblers. But everywhere the effect of dreary uniformity arose from the mobility of the population and the absolute similarity of material conditions.

'When one sees millions of people thinking the same thoughts,' Bryce comments, 'and reading the same books, and perceives that as the multitude grows, its influence becomes always stronger, it is hard to imagine how new points of repulsion and contrast are to arise, new diversities of sentiment and doctrines developed.'

What is apparent in the pages of polite reservation and analysis which the keen English observer wrote, is that he detected after all a notable breakdown in the continuity of culture. Something vital and human had been lost in the transition to the stark industrial society; the moral fiber, the restraining, the saving grace of religious or social impulses such as Europe still contained to a degree—despite her own revolutions and her own terrible transitions—had vanished from America. If you gave prolonged thought to the future, you simply could not discover—during this more ruthless phase of Protestant individualism—what force promised to control, to preserve the country from those moral disasters which menaced all nations in turn. The blessed luck of most Americans was that aside from their business optimism, they were incapable of thinking in terms of the future. . . .

2

There were, to be sure, men and women of the finer grain in this as in other eras, who refused or failed to emigrate to more cultured regions. But they were nearly all beset by the feeling that they were witnessing a time of general coma of the human conscience, and they seem to us to have lived out their days in a world that, if not abysmal and unthinkable to them, seemed like some huge jest or extravagance on the part of the Creator. They loom up for us—certain of these alienated figures—mysteriously, inscrutably, from the great crowd, only to fall back as a tragic and dispersed company, in varying attitudes of resignation or bafflement.

It is a succession of 'eccentrics' that one reviews for the most part, in the group of characters, artists, philosophers, *who stayed, who held their ground*—although the Gilded Age went further in its complacent reasoning and termed them mad. The fatalistic, the silenced, Melville, the outcast Whitman, the mysteriously secluded Emily Dickinson, the painters, Blakelock and Ryder—all, all were insane. And it is only in the light of their extreme detachment from the American order that the frequent and widely recurrent 'madness' of the American artists begins to reveal to us its significant method and its reason.

There were also those who were not to be segregated, either voluntarily or by social opprobrium. Martyrdom was not to their liking, and so they learned to temporize painfully between resignation and unbelief, as did the melancholy Henry Adams, the bewildered and well-intentioned Howells.

And there were those, finally, who became hardened and weather-beaten survivors; who lived to the fullest extent the typical, the unconscionable life of the country, since they had a zest for life on any terms. They learned to 'lie like gentlemen,' as Mark Twain did; or to shoot straight as Ambrose Bierce could. But the results would bring the most curious personal evolution; if one's life were a tissue of lies, or a house of violence and contradictions, one was thrown back in the end upon the horrors of the conscience, and hating his fellows, learned to scorn himself most of all. . . . The strain of morbidity, so typical of American talent, persisted, then, even in those specimens who had clothed themselves protectively with all the varieties of physical prowess and brazenness which the age demanded.

Walt Whitman had survived the great war and now lived in the strange new days as a tranquil and dreamy spectator. He had served for long months in the Union hospitals, tending the sick, receiving the last words of so many dying soldiers. (Surely there was a touch of madness or of religious exaltation in him as he peered into the eyes of dying men and bent over to hear the fading heart-beats.) But now that was all far away, the whole tragic national experience; and he himself seems so greatly altered after his own long illness, with early whitened hair and beard, and his uncanny eyes. There is something very different, something that touches us more than ever, in the later Whitman. In Camden now, secluded from the calumny that his poems had won him, he meditates on the state of things in the country and on its future, preparing all the while a great pamphlet, called *Democratic Vistas*, which he addresses to his people.

It is the heroic quality, the air of speaking from mountain-heights of disinterestedness, that compels us to see in Whitman perhaps the best of character and conscience which the period produces. In the *Vistas* (twenty years after *Leaves of Grass*), with dignity and independence, Whitman chides the republic; and yet at the same time he endeavors to 'say his best' for it, to give expression to its noblest meanings and to inspire it.

Never, he says, was there more hollowness of heart than at present. Genuine belief seems to have left us. No one believes in humanity itself. We live in an atmosphere of hypocrisy, of deceit. The great cities reek with respectable as much as non-respectable robbery and scoundrelism. In business (this all-devouring modern word, business) the one sole object is, by any means, pecuniary gain. The magician's serpent in the fable ate up all the other serpents; and money-making is simply our magician's serpent.

'I say that our New World democracy, however great a success in uplifting the masses, in materialistic development, and in a certain highly deceptive superficial popular intellectuality, is, so far, an almost complete failure in its social aspects, and in really grand religious, moral, literary, and aesthetic results. . . . *It is as if we were somehow endowed with a vast and more and more thoroughly appointed body, and then left with little or no soul.*'

So far it is good; although no one heeds him, none notices him, least of all the great masses whom he loved. Yet with ingenuous confidence he desires to offer a program of amelioration for the benighted age, presenting himself as the *éclaircisseur*, the high 'literatus' of the democracy! He is full of hope—too much hope, one would say—and in his apologia for the violent growth of the republic he abandons himself to a false sentimentalism, a mysticism about pioneers, business, even imperialism; so that those who have followed Whitman blindly have based their faith upon much that is mere vaporing and contradiction.

We find Whitman still believing, with all the fervor of an old libertarian, in the democratic institutions that were so lightly used by cynics and poltroons. He believed in the frontiersmen and celebrated those pioneers who provoked only dismay in Henry James or Henry Adams. They were building an empire, while 'the elder races halted,' and Whitman loved the spectacle with an American's naïve joy in big numbers and wide panoramas.

The myth of the pioneer was to persist for a long time. Doubtless, it was the primitive equality of conditions among which the settlers carved out their rude lives that intrigued democratic thinkers. Whitman imbued the pioneers with a certain poetry, as if the greater part of them were not desperadoes or louts, shiftless, ignoble, or gold-hungry. It was little noted how wasteful the pioneer can be in his preoccupation with immediate gain, or how poorly he builds for the future.

But Whitman believed even in business. He saluted the roaring metropolis of trade, 'million-footed Manhattan.' He saluted science, he hailed the machine. 'A practical, stirring, worldly, money-making, materialistic character' is cheerfully included in his *Vistas,* since he feels that 'the extreme business energy, and this almost maniacal appetite for wealth prevalent in the United States, are parts of amelioration and progress, needed to prepare the very results I demand.' 'I hail with joy,' he continues, 'the oceanic, variegated, intense practical energy, even the business materialism of the current age.'

Whitman sang in the very accents of manifest destiny, desiring that America continue in her paths of expansion to possess herself of new Mexicos, and some day, Panamas and Nicaraguas. . . .

All longing as he was for a domineering America, he would yet liberate our ideas and our arts from the dominance of Europe and a feudal past. In announcing the perspectives of the new literature he was simply expressing what his own poetry had tried to be, the vague, primitive, panoramic chants and catalogues which are the *Leaves of Grass.*

'America demands a poetry that is bold, modern, and all-surrounding and cosmical as she is herself. It must inspire itself with science and the modern. It must bend its vision toward the future, more than the past. Like America it must extricate itself from even the greatest models of the past and have entire faith in itself and the products of the democratic spirit only. Like her it must place in the van, and hold up to all hazards, the banner of the divine pride of man in himself (the radical foundation of the new religion). Long enough have the people been listening to poems in which common humanity, deferential, bends low, humiliated, acknowledging superiors. . . .'

In his infatuation the prophet invokes the shades of Dante, Michael Angelo, and Shakespeare, across the centuries, pleading for their breath of life in our new world's nostrils—'not to enslave us, but to breed a spirit like your own—perhaps (dare we say it?) to destroy what you yourselves have left!'

So firmly persuaded is he of the need of departing from European precedent along the lines of a luminous, new world originality, that he despises 'culture,' or that which he feels passes for it, as exemplified by 'dandies' and '*ennuyés*,' dapper little gentlemen from abroad—'whimpering or crying about something, chasing one aborted conceit after another and forever occupied in dyspeptic amours with dyspeptic women.' He prescribes athletic games, instead.

. . . In fact one could go on enumerating at great length the many points of Whitman's Americanism and come to understand the more clearly why he felt at peace with his fellow men, and not the slightest impulse to decamp.

It strikes us, nevertheless, that Whitman has dismissed the contributions of five centuries of western Europe in a rather cavalier way; that his wish for a 'bold, modern, cosmical' culture, independent of the great world currents, is simply of a piece with his Yankee imperialism. The worst omen of the age, which Whitman speculated upon, was the break from the continuous line of European culture; for the earlier Americans, from Franklin and Jefferson to Emerson, had felt close enough to European thought. 'No one can afford in literature,' wrote Matthew Arnold in a letter concerning Whitman, 'to trade merely on his own bottom and to take no account of what the other ages and nations have acquired; a great original literature America will never get in this way; and her intellect must inevitably consent to come, in a considerable measure, into the European movement. That she may do this and yet be an independent intellectual power, not merely, as you say, an intellectual colony of Europe, I cannot doubt; and it is on her doing this and not on her displaying an eccentric and violent originality that wise Americans should in my opinion set their desires.' The great Victorian critic, despite his slight accent of priggishness, has touched the vulnerable side of the American poet's visions. Still another weak point would be Whitman's celebration of the new world liberties, the democratic spirit of the laws, as against Europe's obsolete discriminations and constraints. Such liberties have more often appeared to us as mere external effects; one had freedom to move rapidly in a world filled with danger and evil, as Whitman himself perceived. The upshot of this unsatisfactory condition—which offered so few spiritual advantages as against Europe's restrictions—was to be the organizing, within a few generations, in the United States, of the most numerous, the most heavily armed, body of police in the whole world. . . .

What passes understanding, finally, is the poet's prophecy of a life of reason, of noble manners, crafts and human arts, which were to emerge from all the materialistic activities and energies he defends. One recalls a vague passage of *Leaves of Grass* in which there is an almost antique vision of a society of beauful men and women, comrades, athletes all, and having a splendid fecundity and imagination. It was a vision, none will fail to recognize, derived more or less from the ancient Greek conceptions of a perfect human society. But how the Yankee tradesman, artisan, or mill-owner of the period we have contemplated with so much misgiving was to become thus sublimated, he fails to explain. As for the pioneer in the west, surely there was little enough poetry in him. It is true that peasants and landholders, when attached to the soil through long centuries, seem to become less earth-bound, and given rather to lovely flights of myth and folk-song. But the American who tilled the land seldom became bound to it; and while his body could roam freely wherever he willed, his mind became prone and rather brutal.

The prophet of Camden might have seen clear portents of conditions unfavorable to his Utopia in the nearly complete ostracism of himself by his countrymen. Though he alone had tried to 'breathe a soul' into the democracy, he might have passed for the most derided and pitiable of village atheists.

There were some who were enchanted by the accents of Whitman and who made pilgrimages to Camden where they might see for themselves the god-like beauty of the man, in his eyes, his bearing, his strange power over those close to him. But they were the very *littérateurs* whom Whitman affected to despise! And though Whitman was truly the spokesman and apologist for his nation, even unto its more bloated vices, he starved at times in Camden and was rescued by the aid of distant European friends, such neophytes of 'culture' as Rossetti, Tennyson, Ruskin, Dowden, Grosart, Gosse.

3

Among the more typical children of the century it is Mark Twain who appeals to us as the most nearly perfect original and model of the local spirit. He was after his own fashion the acknowledged national bard of the United States between 1870 and 1900, as much applauded or consecrated by the *vox populi* as Whitman was ostracized. The comparison with Whitman is indeed highly illuminating. Mark Twain, for a great part of his life at any rate, was even more extravagant than Whitman in celebrating the wonders of nineteenth century progress. He too felt the call of the future. As for the foibles of the present, Mark Twain laughed; and soon the whole nation and even the whole world had caught the infection of his laughter.

Unlike the good gray poet, Mark Twain could not be inspired by the complexion of the world around him to an epic seriousness. At his best he could be funny about it; else he lost the golden touch.

It is significant also that a great many of the notions about American life handed down to our own time—the whole characterization of an industrious, gullible, happy-go-lucky race—were either derived from Mark Twain or compiled by him. Thus, in the course of one of those 'innocent' tours of Europe which he undertook to the delight of his hordes of admirers, the great democratic humorist paused impressively before the Grande Duomo in Florence; prepared to be ravished by the beauty of the cathedral, he finds instead that he can scarcely see it at all for the swarm of stinking beggars who surround him, and he exclaims, 'O sons of classic Italy, is the spirit of enterprise, of self-reliance, of noble endeavor, utterly dead within ye?'

He was speaking in the tones of the 'living, tearing, booming, driving' folk-spirit of America; he was 'showing up' Europe, and the children of the Gilded Age were convulsed at his work.

After the reverent pilgrimages of so many American poets and exquisites to the shrines of art, to the holy places, his was a buffoon's tour. He bore with him his crude skepticism of the sharp salesman or business man; his facile gibes of the tyro played upon everything without mercy; he suspected ruse everywhere, and business dishonesty even on the part of the long-dead Leonardo or Raphael. The *Last Supper* he professed to be unable to see at all, for its blots and scratches; and in the religious paintings of other Italian masters, he perceived not biblical heroes, but the immoral Italian nobles of Borgia's time!

He had used (in *Innocents Abroad*) brickbats on stained glass, and to the minds of his countrymen he had brought down a heap of rubbish. By his aggressive common sense, by his popular derision of culture, and above all his impatience with the traditions, the spirit and meaning, of the past, he became the adored native son, the idol of the day.

Everything about his origins and his career made Mark Twain the archetype of the new American from the west. He was the child of pioneers; he had been one of the many children of a weary, discouraged father and had been reared in one of those shabby towns along the Mississippi, with its litter of rusty cans, rags, garbage, decay. In his youth he had tried all the trades; he had been a printer, a river pilot, a gold-miner in the Sierra Nevadas.

'It was a driving, vigorous, restless population, in those days,' he tells us in *Roughing It*. 'There were none of your simpering, dainty, kid-glove weaklings, but stalwart, muscular, dauntless young braves, brimful of push and energy. . . . For all the slow, sleepy, sluggish-brained sloths stayed at home—you never find that sort of people among pioneers.'

But Mark Twain, though a poor miner, literally struck a bonanza with his pen. From the days of his famous *Jumping Frog* story in 1867, everything he touched turned to gold. After his first public success, he had immediately been taken in hand, as Mr. Van Wyck Brooks relates, and shown the path to fortune and greater royalties even by ministers like Mr. Beecher. The ill-educated frontiersman, who mistrusted his own gifts, became 'respectable' and married an eastern lady of good birth and rich family. Whatever his instincts and sympathies, he would write thenceforth only that which 'paid.' He made the world laugh and millions in gold-pieces flowed through his hands. Fabulously rich, living in the limelight as he had always longed to, sensationally dressed, spending like a Monte Cristo, he was a true, swaggering child of his time. He would risk his quickly gained fortunes in one fantastic enterprise after another, hoping that his mere $100,000 per annum would bring millions; and at moments before disaster overtook him he could cry out in his intoxication, 'Here I am, one of the wealthiest grandees in America—one of the Vanderbilt gang in fact!'

What a curious evolution for a man of letters! From the native surroundings one is infected with such simple ideals! Mark Twain had had a certain imagination and passion in him, and his originality consisted of the usage of these faculties in evoking the native scene, with all its humor, rudeness, contrasts, foibles. But from the beginning he had never really regarded himself as anything but a journalist. He could not be seriously concerned either with the forms or the principles of literary art. He was, as he admitted in his later, more pessimistic vein, a 'sewing-machine' by destiny, and nothing could have permitted him to 'turn out Gobelins.' Knowing thus his own limitations, he displayed a menacing suspicion toward anything which professed to be the result of long and rich reflection, anything which had aesthetic pretensions. Henry James he despised, and nicknamed 'Henrietta-Maria.' He had the pioneer's admiration for brawn and quick results.

Not only did Mark Twain fail to contend with his age; he reveled in it, he frankly enjoyed his ill-fated business schemes, the whirl of great affairs, printing companies, newspapers, machines. He enjoyed 'hob-nobbing with generals, senators, and other humbugs.' He was involved with the Rockefellers, the Rogerses, the nabobs of the time, whose intimacy he was proud to have won; and he frankly liked the power, the great public gestures which his success permitted, just as he liked the banquets he gave in his mansions and the charities he so lavishly distributed. It was the great life, the strenuous life, of the typical American of the century, and it is indisputable that he enjoyed it to the full. In this sense, Mr. Van Wyck Brooks's analysis of his 'self-suppression,' in *The Ordeal of Mark Twain*, is scarcely justified. He had the choice of becoming virtually a pariah, if he spoke out his mind—and his mind was by no means consistently heretical—or of asserting himself grandly in the terms and values of his bourgeois fellows, provided that he never questioned those values. He had chosen. It was the only life that could be lived unless one decamped or became a martyr; and Mark Twain chose to live this life upon a heroic scale. It had its own brutal fascination, its own rewards of self-abandon and the vertigo of power.

Yet in another sense Mr. Brooks's perception of the dualism of Mark Twain's character is keen and just. There is a dualism in all American character: the man who is magisterial at his office desk is a child in the hands of his wife; the man who is cynical in his heart conceals his despair in the circle of his church members. Mark Twain too had generous, courageous impulses and a power of indignation, as he showed during the Dreyfus case. He would declare himself opposed to the 'plutocracy' and in favor of labor unions—but then, was he not also a friend of Uncle Joe Cannon and the Standard Oil chiefs? He had a lighter side, a penchant for high, rollicking mirth, for Gargantuan tales, and for resonant oaths to fill out his sentences with; but he permitted his wife and his dear friend Mr. Howells to censor nearly everything he wrote! And at the very time when he may have been writing certain mildly profane works which now flourish as anonymous masterpieces, attributed to his pen, he publicly abandoned the cause of the Russian revolutionists and its emissary Gorky, because the foreign novelist had been discovered voyaging with another man's wife. . . .

Mark Twain was a divided nature in an even deeper sense. Whosoever looked clearly at the extravaganza of the Gilded Age, with its immitigable farces of Tweeds and Fisks, its orgies of preëmption and bribery, all staged to an accompanying music of patriotism and moral piety, ended by becoming cynical at heart. He might mind his own affairs, practically enough, but if he were not a coated hypocrite, the very act of averting the eyes made him bitter about human nature. In conscious moments one despised his fellows, but was also consumed by self-disgust. As Mark Twain grew old, his fatigue was very apparent; secret writings of an unabated pessimism piled themselves up in his safe for posthumous publication.

Who can forget the pictures of Mark Twain in his old age? The deeply lined face of the great funnyman was one of the most inexplicably tragic of human masks.

4

The genteel literature of the 1870s and 1880s, with its Thomas Aldriches and its Bayard Taylors or its Mary Murfrees and its Margaret Delands, we have mercifully forgotten. There is little that arrests us as we turn the dull pages of this mediocre outpouring of 'local color'—save for an occasional work of the gifted Sarah Orne Jewett, who, for all the prim sparkle of her New England style, had a stiffness, a remoteness of expression that appeals to us more and more as the characteristic touch of her generation.

William Dean Howells, who began late in his career to write the long series of 'realistic' novels (once so greatly overpraised), throned genially among these puritanical, feminine artists, as the well-meaning, cultivated 'dean of American letters.' Having worldly and charming manners as a critic and editor, Howells presided for many years at the literary banquet. But at heart he must have tired much of his rôle; and in the end, by the recently revealed correspondence, he appears to us the most bewildered, the most disabused, the most pathetic, of bystanders. It was cruelly said of Howells that while Henry James went to Europe to study Turgenev and Flaubert, he stayed at home and studied Henry James. . . .

The relationship with James is important; they had had common memories of a literary youth and common longings. The writings of Howells reveal his lifelong subjection to James; the many, voluminous letters, stretching over long years of literary labor, touch on all the issues of the time and all the problems of the art which they faced together.

Howells, as we have seen, had made his way as a poor boy from the middle west to the heart of New England. The members of the cultivated upper class who received him and placed him upon the notable editorial seat left an ineffaceable impression. It was to be a long time before he could bring himself to question them, let alone attack them.

He had resolved at any rate that his place was in America, that his business in life was ultimately to create a mass of novels forming a suggestive satirical painting of American life. On this score there was a long debate, as we have seen, with his expatriated friend, who urged incessantly the dangers of his undertaking and of his post. How often James warned him in letters! Certain of his books are actually written *to* his friend. Henry James urged him to abandon the uniform, monotonous scene, in which transient and unbeautiful conditions triumphed, in which all the 'paraphernalia of civilization' were lacking—so that he might feast his eyes upon the more grateful arrangements of Europe. James was convinced, moreover, that Howells was beset by all the perils which he had escaped from. He would be buried under what Whitman called 'countless masses of adjustments'; he would hold himself in check too long by the maneuvers of compromise, missing forever the golden opportunity to live fully and freely in his own light; to live at least in the illusion of freedom!

But Howells held his ground. An essayist by nature and self-culture, and if not a critic, at least a professor of good literature who could distinguish and encourage talent—Howells really went astray in the novel. He became the champion of realism long after Henry James himself had forsaken it in his own more intricate evolution. But his realism consisted merely of an avoidance of arbitrary or improbable episode, of a duplication of the exact length, propriety, and dullness of middle-class American conversation. And so the *Hazard of New Fortunes,* for all its close description of American business careers and manners, is lacking in intensity or precipitation. The New England domestic drama, *A Modern Instance* (once likened to Tolstoy's work), is no less a failure for much the same reasons. For, early in life, Howells had recoiled from certain sordid experiences and resolved that 'the more smiling aspects of life are the more American'; so that he denied himself that thumping on the bass strings which typifies the prose of a Zola and a Maupassant, and often makes works of exact realism memorable or powerful.

Henry James had a persistent, bitter sense of what his friend 'might have been' in a more favorable situation, filled with more inspiring impressions and associations. He felt keenly the want of relief and force in the man's work. How can you go on painting American life, he writes in effect, in such *fatal* colors? How, my dear Howells, can you occupy yourself so much with people whom one mortally dislikes?

Possessing a greater charity and altruism toward his fellow beings and a less pure attitude toward his art than did James in his later manner, Howells responded at times to local problems in a spirit of active protest. But it was a greatly tempered protest. The opposition of the *illuminati*, of the intellectual minority, rarely raised its head in this violent era. True, during the Haymarket riots of Chicago in 1887, when the press and the whole country called for the blood of the seven anarchists, Howells did write a letter of beautiful indignation to the Governor of Illinois; but no preachers or authors, either from Boston or New York, followed him in this cause, and the fruitless effort was speedily hushed up. (Likewise, in 1898, William James spoke at a meeting of protest against the Spanish-American War; but all such outbursts were soon thought of only as *moments of folly* on the part of well-intentioned, respectable philosophers, who rarely again exposed themselves to the obloquy of lost causes.) Generous and kind as he could be, Howells wrote from no depth of conviction; he celebrated or attacked no institution with a fixed moral passion. When we compare the realists and social critics of Howells' type to great Europeans who had been attacking society for two centuries, we become painfully aware of their timidity. In the satirical novel, *Democracy,* which Henry Adams is supposed to have written, one of the characters makes the bitter comment: 'You are just like the rest of us. You grow six inches high, and then you stop. Why will not somebody grow to be a tree and cast a shadow?'

Even when Howells professes to doubt, to abhor, the civilization of his time and to long for a *real equality,* he admits his own uncertainties. He confesses, in a letter to Henry James, 'I should hardly like to trust pen and ink with all the audacity of my social ideas.' When, in *A Traveler from Altruria,* he advances his mildly Utopian concoctions, he does this, again, most apologetically, as if to say: 'You must really forgive me these fancies. I am a queer old man who, after fifty years of optimistic content, now suspects that there is much evil in the world. . . .'

His humility is unmistakable. He says on one occasion in a rather touching letter: 'I am not sorry for having wrought in common, crude material so much; that is the right American stuff; and perhaps hereafter when my din is done, if any one is curious to know what that noise was, it will be found to have proceeded from a small insect which was scarping about on the surface of our life and trying to get into its meaning for the sake of the other insects, larger or smaller. Such has been my unconscious work; consciously, I was always, as I still am, trying to fashion a piece of literature out of the life next at hand.'

As a bewildered old gentleman, speaking discreetly now and then in the great magazines for the great Russians, or for Henry James or the persecuted Thomas Hardy, Howells waited dubiously for the social revolution so vaguely anticipated, while continuing to wear in the meantime 'my fur-lined overcoat and living in all the luxury my money can buy.'

5

Was an eternity of Grants and Garfields and Jay Goulds conceivable? Henry Adams asked himself toward 1870. He had returned to Washington some years after the Civil War, and what he had seen, what he had felt, may be read in the amazing social document which he has left us, *The Education of Henry Adams.*

Unlike the other sanguine, positivistic children of the Gilded Age, Adams's thoughts were obsessed with the idea of the imminent ruin of the world. There is something curiously decadent about Henry Adams himself: he is a scholar and yet a dilettante; his curiosities are persistent, insatiable, and drive him in a great many strange directions, carry him even to the farthest corners of the world. One may see the Faustian drama in his poignant search for ideas, for an absolute science of human history; he pursues literature, politics, history, in turn; then he plunges into the modern scientists, the Lyells and Darwins who have electrified the nineteenth century, only to arrive at the conviction that science is hopeless. Nothing could ever illuminate the darkness of the universe; nor was there any hope of amelioration for men, if you confined your interest to the human world. Greed and fear were the strongest impulses of the 'gold-bugs,' the automatons of the republic. Perhaps in the end men would take a circular course from a paradise of usurers, through communism, to religion? . . . Yet Adams was not outwardly bitter: he had vowed himself to silence and good humor, foreseeing martyrdom for himself (and he had no taste for it) if he spoke his mind.

In his youth Henry Adams had written to his brother Charles Francis: 'What we want is a school. We want a national set of young men like ourselves or better to start new influences, not only in politics, but in literature, in law, in society, and throughout the whole social organism of the country—a national school of our own generation.'

These interesting hopes, conceived under the influences of his British and European sojourn, had visioned a gathering up of so much random, insulated work that was being done for temporary or personal purposes in a combined action toward unselfish ends. By his exposures of Jay Gould's famous 'corner in gold,' by his attacks on the politicians involved in the corrupt Erie Railroad affair, Adams had won some reputation and had taken steps in the direction of the public service he believed in. He had later become the historian of the heroic age of American politics by his great volumes on Hamilton and Jefferson. Now a historian was the President of France; a brilliant Jew, combining the gifts of the novelist, the parliamentarian, and the dandy, reigned over the British Empire. What career was there for Adams, subtle, curious, unsatisfied spirit, whose unrest was so symptomatic?

Nothing seems more futile, in the retrospect of his memoirs, than the years which, clinging to Washington as a possible vantage point, he passed as the 'stable-mate,' the adviser, of politicians. He had refused dubious appointments but hovered about the environs of Lafayette Square, rallying, preaching to influential friends in office. He had theories, natural to an Adams, of civic duty, of social virtue, of the good life; and he sought—without too much ardor, one feels—to disseminate them, at a time when every branch of government functioned, apparently, only to aid the taking of money from some one else through the processes of law.

With the aid of his accomplished wife, Adams kept open house in F Street; during the '70s and '80s there was nowhere in the United States such a 'salon.' Every one of 'quality' passed through it. The gifted John Hay and the scientist Clarence King, together with the Adamses, formed a witty and mocking circle, joined from time to time by artists such as Lafarge and Saint Gaudens, philosophers like William James, men of letters like Howells, as well as foreign dignitaries. The memoirs and correspondence of this rather illuminated if unenergetic group are touched with charm and pathos.

Henry James in his brief visit to Washington had declared the society of Hay, King, and Adams to be the most entertaining in America. Solicited by certain transient hopes, his interest had revived for a moment, and he thought that here at least he might be something. 'If I were to abide by my vanity only, I should never return to that Europe which ignores me.' But he knew better, or at any rate he loved Europe more than his vanity.

What James would soon have perceived was that the promising, the brilliant, Washington group were glow-worms drenched in a surrounding darkness. They trembled at times for their very safety. Stirred by the great Cleveland steel strike, John Hay wrote a mediocre novel, *The Breadwinners*, which was but a specious defense of the rights of property; and Henry Adams wrote a satire of the political arena, *Democracy*—yet both authors remained anonymous, not daring to acknowledge their work. Whatever their dissent might be, whatever their points of superiority, nothing is more suggestive of the helplessness and the great uncertainty of the American intellectuals than the anonymity they clung to.

The rôle of the man of enlightenment, the man of sensibility, in American life, was to be a pitiable one for the next fifty years. In the last analysis the intellectuals of the time could not have furnished leadership for the nation, since they were cut off by their sympathies, by their ideals, from the whole crusade of the people toward the mountains of gold and the fields of oil. The assertion of their individualisms—if they had but dared—the urging of individual tastes and principles against the absolute uniformity imposed by the system of mechanical progress called manifest destiny, would have been a form of betrayal. 'A vast, unconscious conspiracy,' writes Mr. Van

Wyck Brooks, 'actuated all America at this time against the creative spirit.' It would be far more accurate, however, to regard the mild *illuminati* of the Gilded Age, who invoked the creative spirit, as passing conspirators themselves. Those who longed for an aesthetic and moral perfection simply opposed the voiced will of the people. They were in a highly anomalous position; they were alienated, and their gentle idealisms had lost all touch with the realities of the time.

By 1887 Henry Adams had touched depths of despair. His rejection of democracy is vivid in the pages of *The Education*, which are the most tragic record of human frustration ever written by an American. In his extremity, the historian-philosopher withdrew from the world and devoted himself to studies in mediaeval Christian art. He had come to doubt whether mankind ever progressed within the limits of recorded history, or ever will progress or do anything but retrograde! [2] And to doubt Progress was to betray the folk-spirit of all America. He believed, moreover, that the highest terms in which 'the intensity of the vital energy' of a given time could be measured were art and religion. And in the United States these impulses had reached their lowest ebb. (In quest of pure and primitive art and feeling, Adams, together with John Lafarge, set off

[2] The extremely curious *Letter to Teachers of American History* (1908), reveals him as a predecessor of the organic notion of culture, a prophet of 'decline' like the German, Spengler.

on a voyage as far as the magical recently discovered Japan, to 'find Nirvana. . . .') The modern world, as Adams saw it, could only pervert and degrade such instincts. Measured by his art and his religion, man had only moved backward in the thousand years since Chartres and St. Thomas Aquinas. So that when Adams' wandering trail led him at last to the mystical certitudes of *Mont Saint-Michel and Chartres*—the great wistful study of the twelfth century worship of the Virgin as sublimated sex—he published his book privately, desiring that it be read only by the 'limited number of survivors, the one in a thousand of born artists.'

Men had ceased to worship sex, either as Venus or the Virgin. Americans were essentially sexless; and the call of the American girl (of the magazine covers) was not that of the mysterious fecundity which ruled nature in the minds of the Middle Ages. It was something more trivial: in his novel, *Democracy*, he had hinted that the American beauty bursts into her 'golden smile' largely to show her perfect teeth.

A great revelation had finally come to Adams, in a visit to one of the industrial expositions of the time, when he stood in the hall of dynamos. The dynamo became a symbol of infinity; *and men worshiped the forty-foot dynamos*—which seemed to render the whole planet itself unimpressive with its old-fashioned, deliberate cycles—much as the early Christians felt the Cross!

6

It was a world in which it was dangerous to fail and equally dangerous to 'succeed.' And if his sensibility was the dominant part of him, greater than that of Mark Twain or Whitman, the artist found recourse only in an interior life of a terrible isolation.

I have spoken of Melville's self-willed obscurity, but there is an even more poignant instance, if that is possible, of one of the true lyric geniuses of the age, the most naturally gifted of American poets, living unknown both to the world and to other poets for a long half-century.

Emily Dickinson, who was born in 1833 and died in 1886, knew the cloistered destiny of the votaress. The conjecture and incredulousness with which her long-hidden poems were received in 1890 can only arouse our indignation today. To have withheld her literature from her contemporaries strikes us as a severe judgment of her age and a profoundly right one. For everything that she wrote was posthumous and clearly designed to appear after her death. In the couplet which introduces her volume she says:

> This is my letter to the world
> Which never wrote to me.

It was a poetry as wildly free in its imagination, as primitive and pure in language, as widely divorced from conventional meters and images, as that of Blake. And the poet, like certain other abundantly talented Americans, was rated a little mad by the literary pedantry. . . .[3]

For most of her haunting and enchanted life, Emily Dickinson scarcely ever stirred beyond the precincts of the great house and the hedged garden at Amherst. She lived intensely, unstintedly, with her personal God, who bore all the colors of eternity—'eternity which sweeps round me like a sea.' The power of her vision, the sheer naked passion of her appeals and communions, were in the manner of some possessed mediaeval saint rather than of the reasoning New England conscience. She worshiped and sang to the Spirit whom she saw everywhere about her, as the aborigine sees spirits in every animate form—but with all her senses of sight, sound, smell, touch. Her trances were touched to such a degree with fear, violence, cruelty, or even flagellation, that one is minded of the religious experiences which William James later dissected, and suspects inevitably the working of a sublimated sex instinct such as a later psychiatry presumes. But however we may

[3] As late as 1915, Professor F. L. Pattee wrote, in *American Literature Since 1870,* of Emily Dickinson's poems: 'They are mere conceits, vague jottings of a brooding mind . . . crudely wrought (and like their author's letters . . .) colorless and for the most part lifeless. They should have been allowed to perish as their author intended.' (!!!) It is obvious that Emily Dickinson did not intend her work to perish. Dr. Pattee is misguided. Moreover, up to the tenth edition of his otherwise useful compendium, he had not retracted his stupid appraisal.

choose to characterize the poetess—and here is the danger of Freudianism—it does not mitigate the force and the quality of her perceptions.

In her youth, Emily Dickinson had enjoyed the world ingenuously. Strangely, puzzlingly beautiful (though of an unconventional mold), pale and with piercing, disconcerting eyes, she had had admirers and had not sought to avoid the society and the simple merry-making of the old college town. Then the wounding shock had come; her passion, which one feels almost livid at every stage, turned from the forbidden, socially denied lover, to one whom she might love boundlessly. In the transfiguration of her desires she renounced the world outside, to live chastely, but with a tremendous animation, within the walls of her soul.

She began to write during the Civil War. 'I had a terror since September I could tell to none,' she says in one of her letters, 'and so I sing, as the boy does of the burying-ground, because I am afraid.'

Her letters themselves, like her poems, are of an unequaled purity and freshness and are among the most fantastic in the language. This New England maid wrote as if the language were in its morning, as if it were the time of Kyd or Ben Jonson or John Webster. Thus: 'If I tried to thank you my tears would block my tongue.' And she explains further her impulse to poetry: 'My dying tutor told me that he would like to live till I had been a poet, but Death was much of mob as I could master then. And when far afterward, a sudden light on orchards, or a new fashion in the wind troubled attention, I felt a palsy, here, the verses just relieve.'

In short, the lyric filled an immediate, overwhelming need, and arose in her with that lack of pretense, or self-consciousness, which 'primitive' artists exhibit in the making of their superb totems and masks. Indeed, Emily Dickinson, in her lonely corner, was clairvoyant to such a degree, she saw and sensed so much, that to entrust her amazing observations, aphorisms, and images to her prosy neighbors would have invited suspicion and perhaps repressions!

'I would eat evanescence slowly . . .' she says. 'I hear today for the first time the river in the trees.'

And so her poems, in a perfect hand, are confided to her letters and her journal. Only three or four were published, anonymously, during her lifetime, and these were secured by friends after great effort, and even through ruse. Her poems were 'tossed off'; they were the breath of her inner life, which she would neither explain nor defend. She had no wish to proselytize; she had no ambition for literary glory!

She felt her largest need to be that of living with 'the unknown,' in a supreme detachment. 'You ask me of my companions. Hills, sir, and the sundown and a dog large as myself, that my father bought me.' It was just as well, since there were naturally good people like the Bostonian, Colonel T. W. Higginson, her discoverer, who sought to *correct* her cunningly irregular verses, 'to lead her in the direction of rules and traditions.' May they be forgiven! But at any rate, she preferred her 'barefoot rank,' as she put it cryptically; and she shunned men and women, because 'they talk of hallowed things, aloud, and embarrass my dog.'

Moreover, none of these poor people could have possibly communicated with her mind. If Emily Dickinson encountered a new flower, or a strong book, she became drunk!

'If I read a book and it makes my whole body so cold no fire can ever warm me, I know that is poetry. If I feel physically as if the top of my head were taken off, I know that is poetry. These are the only ways I know it. Is there any other way?'

The sources of harmony and joy which she had found in her *animated* universe (in the metaphysical sense), with its personal, poetic God, she knew were not for the rest of the world, and were denied by it. It could never comprehend her and her spiritual problems. She would pass for mad.

> Assent and you are sane—
> Demur—you're straightway dangerous
> And handled with a chain.

She had, then, the hills, the orchard, and above all the sky. She had Sir Thomas Browne and Revelation and Keats and Mr. Ruskin. The rest she abandoned, with a charming wisdom, and secretly mocked—duties, money, possessions, all the grave and busy problems of an ill-favored time.

It was not as if she had no choice. Do not think that she did not glimpse the great outside world in the activities of the lovely old village, with its 'births and deaths, spites, ministerial side-takings, early tea-parties, religious revivals in season, or the panic of unexpected relatives driving up for uninvited visits.' She renounced this as she renounced all partiality for the material world. She suspected that *people lived without thoughts*—and their life seemed intolerable. With marvelous intuition and as if from far off she had diagnosed the great default of her times.

'Won't you please tell me,' she writes during one of those periods of legal and regularly recurring uproar which mark American history, 'when you answer my letter, who the candidate for President is? . . . I don't know anything more about the affairs in the world than if I were in a trance.'

7

A view of the artistic period that closed toward 1900 could little afford to ignore Ambrose Bierce, who appeals to us nowadays as one of the most amusing, devilish, and perplexing characters of the dark era. As the years pass his spectacular and little-known career becomes almost legendary. It is a career that suggests forcibly the queer exposures, the queer influences, the still queerer evolution, that a man of letters might suffer in the United States. When we associate Bierce's life with his time and his milieu (the more violent stage of manifest destiny), we note certain impressive 'protective resemblances.' The idea then forms itself that in a marked degree this career exemplifies the art of living with violence. . . .

Bierce was an irrepressible, mordant wit; he was a hard drinker; he was a furious polemicist; he was a 'nihilist,' in short. One estimated that he had seen a great deal of the world, that he had lived in the gambling hells of mining towns, that he had killed men.

Ambrose Bierce's heresies, combined with his fantastic temper, were destined to place him beyond the 'Draconian moral code' of the time. An invalid, and widely hated, he lived for many years in a kind of Olympian isolation on the mountains of the Pacific coast. He was, as he liked to call himself, 'a lone wolf.' Despite his ailments he enjoyed a terrible physical strength and great physical beauty, which brought him the devotion of men and the surrender of women. He was strikingly tall, with a great blond mane, and shaggy yellow eyebrows under which the piercing blue eyes flashed. For a long time, during the '80s and '90s, his vigorous, brisk shadow brandished itself weirdly. Uncommon and tragic experiences marked his writings; and by compliment literature colored his adventures strongly—above all the beautiful last one, in which Bierce, very ancient but still hale, wandered off with a horse and revolver to join the Mexican revolution in 1913, and to disappear from sight forever.

'You must try to forgive my obstinacy in not "perishing" where I am,' he wrote to a friend in the United States. 'I want to be where something worth while is going on. Most of what is going on in your own country is extremely distasteful to me. . . . It is better than dying in bed, or falling down the cellar stairs. I am leaving the field to the younger authors.'

The last letters, by their tone, candidly anticipate death. But the field being abandoned had scarcely ever been possessed. Ambrose Bierce had enjoyed only an 'underground reputation.' His superb *Tales of Soldiers and Civilians* had been refused by all the editors and publishers in the country and owed their appearance to the solicitude of a few friends. He had long before (when he was not much over forty) ceased all serious effort at writing, save that of the necessary journalism which sustained him. He had survived himself too long, and even his own sacred rage; all was superannuated, and now, as intransigeant ghost, he renounced the world which had so little accepted him.

Like Mark Twain, Ambrose Bierce was the son of poor settlers. With Indiana volunteers he had entered the Union army and fought during the whole Civil War. For his courage he had been distinguished with severe wounds and the brevet of a major. After Appomattox, he had pushed west with the demobilized hordes that issued from the armies, a pioneer in his turn, dreaming of gold or sensational turns of fortune. He had been nearest to gold when he had held a clerical post at the mint of San Francisco, and by his address he had won the hand of Mollie Day, a reigning California belle.

In those days Bierce had loved the port of San Francisco, and although he did not fall in with fortune, and he was soon—it is sad to say—separated from his pretty wife, he was already accepted among the curious, congenial circle of western bohemians, those 'Argonauts' who, having missed the golden fleece, sought other incommensurables in the arts of drinking, conversation, and letters. Joaquin Miller, Adah Isaacs Menken, Bret Harte, Mark Twain, Artemus Ward, Charles Stoddard, and other characters formed for a time an odd provincial company which treated itself with that provincial seriousness typical of scenes remote from the main currents of the world. They were 'originals' in the sense that they crudely reflected local habits and prejudices and did much to propagate the works of 'local color' which so delighted the Gilded Age.

Bierce was known as a redoubtable journalist who was always ready to exchange shots down the street with an offended critic, in accordance with the charming ethics of the region. The moral code had been set by brawny and desperate bravos such as were described in *Roughing It,* and a man who would survive for the sake of *belles-lettres* must be ready to shed the gore of his fellow men. And there was a primitive beauty to be felt from the heights of the Sierra Nevadas, despite the ramshackle wooden-frame architecture of the '50s which still characterized San Francisco, despite the sprawling mine settlements, so soon abandoned, preternaturally rusty and old. A man could become a poet, among these savage and grandiose conditions, especially if he were a big man and a dead shot like Bierce. It was an odd fact, of course, that poets of the far west—like Joaquin Miller and his great sombrero—extended themselves in a diffuse bombast which only amused the poets of plainer lands. But Ambrose Bierce was saved from all this and was enabled to dedicate himself to a more informed and craftsmanlike art.

At some moment of ripening consciousness, when he was not quite thirty, Bierce resolved to see the world, and in 1871 we find him transported to London, where he lived for five years. He had become, like Henry James, one of the latter-day 'pilgrims,' and had felt himself in England close to the 'fountainhead of Anglo-Saxon culture.' It was not the dignified world in which James and Lowell moved that Bierce was introduced to, but rather the impecunious, the jovial and garrulous one of Grub Street, which starved and guzzled and ground out 'copy' and yet remained infinitely more civilized than it was possible to be anywhere in America. For years, then, Ambrose Bierce lived in the company of the somewhat raffish celebrities of Bohemia, men like Mayne Reid, Sala, and the younger Tom Hood, who contributed to *Fun* and other light periodicals.

'We worked too hard,' he relates, 'we dined too well, frequented too many clubs, and went to bed too late in the forenoon. In short, we diligently, conscientiously, and with a perverse satisfaction burned the candle of life at both ends and in the middle.'

In view of his delight in London life and English manners, as well as in the company and the alehouses neighboring Fleet Street, it is evidently a matter of chance or necessity that brings him back to San Francisco. One wonders what long exposure to European conditions and the contact of keen or sympathetic minds would have done for his talents. For he had been awakened by his voyages, and some time afterward had begun to write those much-polished and pointed tales, with their surprising note of synthetic, of artfully directed, tragedy. Would they have been passed over in silence by the sophisticated Pre-Raphaelites? Would they not have been welcomed in Paris, where the star of Maupassant was about to rise?

Returning to America, Bierce found little to his liking. He found himself moving counter to the conventions of the age. He despised the fictions of the magazines, which were dominated by the faded New England school. He had returned with the conviction that Henry James had gained in Paris: that art and morality were two separate things. Above all he would not moralize; certain forms of sentimentality had been stamped out of him by his experience, and he had acquired a sardonic detachment toward human nature that was not far removed from misanthropy.

The Civil War had been his largest adventure, and so his first stories were drawn from this period. They are, for the reader, among the most trying war stories ever written, since they are utterly lacking in pity, and not only shrink from no detail of carnage and horror, but actually seek out such effects of the elaborate macabre as may ornament the author's scheme. The form of Bierce's short story is based on the 'final twist' which Poe largely originated; and one may readily see how skillfully all the gratuitous tricks of frustration or horror, in the game of war which pits human chance against natural force, are employed through Bierce's technique. There is an unvarying fatality: each of the individuals singled out for courage or cowardice moves inevitably toward his last hour, which is generally decorated with the grotesque colors of the charnel house. One recalls the picture, for instance, of a battery whose single remaining gun, for want of water, is swabbed from a pool of blood, so that the cannon appears to bleed at the mouth! Hundreds of such bloody fantasies had imprinted themselves upon Bierce's mind as his chief memory of glorious battlefields. But the power of Bierce's war stories—probably the only great stories that came out of that war—resides not in their obvious realism but in their remarkable economy and condensation. Bierce's style permits of no superfluous language; it evokes images and movements through the unconventional use of verbs rather than adjectives, arrived at by the most deliberate kind of selection. In *The Horseman in the Sky* the qualities are almost sculptural: one sees the Rebel observer on his high bluff, who has been reached by a single shot, caught in mid-air as he descends upon his steed in a perfect arc against a marvelous landscape. And in *Chickamauga* there is the picture of the lost child, deaf and mute, playing with his wooden sword, who leads an army of wounded soldiers, crawling noiselessly, down a reddened hillside toward water. All these moments of instability—as in a dance—of ingenious, dire paradox on the part of the universe, seem to appeal to Bierce not merely as sadist, but through his love for the purely kaleidoscopic, through his perception of form and mysterious beauty in each accidental effect or light. To the well-worn themes of 'honor, devotion, courage,' Bierce adds little. He cared little enough for the issues of the war. Hating men in their civilized rôles, he found them more entertaining in the primitive ones of the battlefield, where tedious pretexts were all stripped away, and the human passions, the human drama, were all concentrated for him in a single illuminated moment or image.

If the synthetically horrible war stories were destined to go unread by his generation, how much more distasteful would be those which played with the supernatural and the ghostly. This was another side of Bierce's talent; and one feels how dominantly intellectual the appeal of mystery, of death, of ghostly antics and coincidences, was to this essentially self-conscious artist.

The supernatural must be seen, in the end, as the favored atmosphere of American literature. It is as if the realities of the diurnal native scene imposed upon the most gifted writers a need for escape. What else explains the somber preoccupation of Hawthorne, Poe, Melville, Bierce, Lafcadio Hearn, and even Henry James in a later phase? There is also the added attraction, to the inventive literary artists, that the more preposterous incident is susceptible of use within arbitrary patterns; so that symbols of ideas may be created, as in Hawthorne, or perfect mathematical relationships, as in Poe.[4] Indeed, the American strain begins to appear no longer a barbarian, happy and headlong one. Only Whitman could make poems out of the statistics of expansion or prosperity; and in Whitman the sense for perfect detail, for finished surface, was at a low ebb as compared with his will for a colossal program and framework.

In the genre of the supernatural, Bierce intrigues us most of all by his occasional gropings in the subconscious mind. *The Death of Halpin Frayser*, whose theme verges on the Oedipus complex, is clearly an example of writing which is two generations in advance of its time. The story opens with the hero wandering lost in the great redwood forests of California and falling asleep, by an odd coincidence, across the grave of his mother, whom he seeks among the living and who, he believes, is searching for him. 'In these two romantic natures was manifest in a signal way,' Bierce says, 'that neglected phenomenon, the dominance of the sexual element in all the relations of life, strengthening, softening, and beautifying even those of consanguinity.'

The man dreams: all the foliage of the woods is touched with blood; he hears the sound of distant laughter, of invisible existences forming 'a monstrous conspiracy against his body and soul.' Vainly he

[4] The Americans seemed much more notable for their technical inventive genius than for intellectual or emotional range.

tries by tracing life backward in memory to reproduce the moment of his sin! His voice babbles brokenly: 'I will not submit unheard. There may be powers that are not malignantly traveling this accursed road. I shall leave them a record and an appeal. I shall relate my wrongs, the persecutions that I endure. . . .' He dips a twig into a pool of blood and begins to write rapidly a poem of protest and self-justification. (It is an excellent poem, drawing upon the genius of great dead poets, as one may in a dream.) All the business related has in reality taken but the fraction of a minute: the interval in which some invisible power has touched the sleeper's lids and waked him with the name of his mother on his lips, '*Catherine Larue!*'—and then the succeeding one, in which a maniac, the lover of his mother, leaps from the shadow and strangles him. Yet the tale has the most exact dissociations of the subconscious fantasy, which Bierce understood so well, and is rich with the profoundest suggestions. The stately sentences of the close reproduce in their cadences the rise and fall of unearthly laughter:

'There came to them out of the fog—seemingly from a great distance—the sound of a laugh, a low, deliberate, soulless laugh, which had no more of joy than that of a hyena night-prowling in the desert: a laugh that rose by slow gradations, louder and louder, clearer, more distinct and terrible, until it seemed barely outside the narrow circle of their vision. . . . As it had grown out of silence, so now it died away; from a culminating shout which had seemed almost in their ears, it drew itself away into the distance, until its falling notes, joyless and mechanical to the last, sank to silence at a measureless remove.'

The briefest study of Bierce's writings is enough to reveal a powerful imaginative talent, a mind of many curiosities, of uncertain education, which nevertheless longs for discipline and eagerly pursues for a time its ideal of perfection in language and form. . . . *Then the pursuit lags, and is given over.* After the two or three volumes, filled with small, pure jewels, the rest of the Collected Works drops into a chaotic miscellany, of lampoons, epigrams, vignettes, tidbits, all the leavings of a scattered, diverted effort. Instead of developing from the limited form of the short tale to work on a larger scale, Ambrose Bierce *soon ceased all serious literary effort.* The effect, for us, is of some dismembered torso, of a beautiful intention or design, found among the flimsy ruins and rubbish of the Gilded Age.

Ambrose Bierce was prompted logically to renounce literature in favor of life, one might say, of a life of action. But whether he renounced literature or in turn life itself—as he did twenty years later by his fatal journey into Mexico—there was almost no stir of sympathy or curiosity excited in his contemporary world.

All the second half of his life remains obscured by contradictory reports of confused, random movements; he preferred to mystify his acquaintances, no doubt, because he was conscious of the censure that might be invoked for him. The evidence impresses us with a character resolved to develop his own personal differences at all costs, to explore to the limits his own nature rather than conform to the standards of the crowd. We gain at the same time the sense of a tormented struggle for equilibrium, under the dire conditions, a struggle in which he is to be the loser, tangibly—by tragic personal experiences, by the diversion of his natural gifts—and the winner, only in certain intangibles, of the interior life which can never be scrutinized or measured.

In the painful, prolonged search for equilibrium there is the lesson—if we may clutch at it—of Bierce's strange career. He was beset, he was opposed inevitably, by so much that enraged, oppressed, humiliated, that there was no chance to acquire the tranquillity that he needed, the knowledge of himself and his powers, until it was almost too late.

We can easily imagine how much he was vexed by the spirit of bigoted Puritanism before which Mark Twain and Howells yielded. 'Who am I to be casting the first stone!' he would say. And indeed the pattern of his domestic life must have been exceedingly curious for those privileged to behold it. Even as an old man, chained to the mountains by his rheumatism, he must descend to the valleys in quest of drink and women. Bierce, related one of his friends, 'found his main happiness, intermittent as that may have been, in the society of the woman for whom he cared most at the time. . . .' And it is disclosed further that though he was discreet, his intrigues incurred serious danger, necessitated long journeys to distant cities in his ripe old years. We are told that Bierce corresponded voluminously with his chosen ladies and lived in horror of the publication of his letters, foreseeing after death a disastrous epilogue of duels and broken homes!

The comedy of morals in his time, as he intimated in certain digressions, was so painful that an intelligent man could only hold his tongue.

'This is not a love story,' he wrote in *The Realm of the Unreal*. 'I am no story-teller, and love as it is cannot be portrayed in a literature dominated and enthralled by the debasing tyranny which "sentences letters" in the name of the Young Girl. Under the Young Girl's blighting reign—or rather under the rule of those false ministers of the Censure who have appointed themselves to the custody of her welfare—

love

veils her sacred fires,
And, unawares, Morality expires

famished upon the sifted meal and distilled water of a prudish purveyance.'

Bierce refrained from writing on love, undoubtedly to our loss, for he may have been, very likely, one of the true artists of love.

Added to the quarrel with Puritanism there was, for Bierce, the even more momentous quarrel with the idea of Progress. He was one of those men, as Santayana has phrased it, who though born a conservative and drawn to poetic subtlety or gay passions, had, nevertheless, the categorical excellence of work, growth, enterprise, reform, and prosperity dinned in his ears. Every door was opened in this direction and shut in the other. So that he must either 'fold up his heart and wither in a corner—or fly to Oxford or Florence, or Montmartre, to save his soul, or perhaps not to save it.'

To the sardonic mind of Ambrose Bierce the world was bad enough and could only be made worse. 'I care nothing for principles,' he would say; 'they are lumber and rubbish. . . . And as to sin, that has an abundance of expounders and is already wicked, whereas the sinner cometh up as a flower every day, fresh, ingenuous, and inviting.' He despised the socialism which made converts steadily in his time. The poor, he believed, wished only to be richer, not better. And on the other hand he would curse the 'smug-wump,' Carnegie, for a moralizing hypocrite. Such tactics, it will be perceived, won him no friends in either camp.

During his long residence in or near California he learned to detest the limited world of San Francisco. It was 'a moral penal-colony . . . a paradise of ignorance, anarchy, and general yellowness'; it needed, in his estimation, only another quake, another whiff of fire, and more than all else, 'a steady trade-wind of grapeshot.' It was as corrupt as London, but there was no good conversation, there were no good manners, society, culture.

The popular literature of the time was composed of those stories of 'local color' which a Bret Harte, a Cable, a Mark Twain, made universal; and in this tendency toward the use of slang Bierce saw the leveling and even degrading influence of democracy. The talk of ignorant persons misusing their own language had value and interest for nobody, he held; and it were better for authors if 'instead of writing things "racy of the soil" they would till it. . . .'

Ultimately, he evolved out of his prejudices of a gentleman of the old school, out of his contempt for progress, what may roughly be called a philosophy of aristocracy. He even went so far at one time as to outline, though with his tongue in his cheek, his model of intellectual perfection, a kind of program for the élite:

'This fortunate youth with the brilliant future should learn to take comprehensive views, hold large convictions, and make wide generalizations. He should, for example, forget that he is an American and remember that he is a man. . . . To local standards of right and wrong he should be civilly indifferent. In the virtues, so called, he should discern only the rough notes of a general expediency. . . . He should free himself of all doctrines, theories, etiquettes, politics, simplifying his life and mind, attaining to clarity with height. To him a continent should not seem too wide, nor a century long. And it would be needful that he know and have an ever-present consciousness that this is a world of fools and rogues, consumed with vanity, selfish, false, cruel, cursed with illusions—frothing mad.'

Holding such views, it was inevitable that all doors to the 'free' organs of opinion and literature should be effectually closed to him. At every point, the prevailing tastes, whatever they were—of frigid spinsters or complacent tradesmen—tended to reduce such a man to the minimum of creative effort and drive most of this underground. He might conceive a heroic program for himself; but there were no men of his own stature; no authorities lifted their solicitous voices for him; none, in fact, would read his melancholy prose which grew entertaining only at the expense of his fellow men. Immensely skeptical,

Bierce could see as clearly as any one else how the values he cherished were doomed.

Yet if we lament the outcome of this conflict, the thwarted career, the meager production, we must admit that there was all the rest of life left for the man, if he but had the zest for it on its own violent terms. Bierce had this, and to such a degree that we readily understand his dislike for literary circles and his indifference to the failure of his writings. Looking clearly about him, beneath the surface, he saw only anarchy, the semi-legal anarchy of the steam-power age and the pioneer society. If one did not flee the country, or remain slave, automaton, 'sewing-machine,' he might persist hardily, once he had made his renunciations—another such anarchic type as was produced by the anarchic struggle of the time!

Ambrose Bierce became, as we have noted, a journalist. He despised newspapers, but he appraised the writing of books for *hoi polloi* of literacy as lower than horse-stealing. He was no ordinary journalist. He took pleasure in eternal polemics, in fighting, cracking skulls, smashing reputations according to all the rules of the sensational yellow press. Once he had abandoned literature, he found for himself in the world of action the rôle of adversary to the great Southern Pacific trust. The millions of a Collis Huntington could not bribe this man-without-principles. For long years Bierce directed his finest effort to inventing abuse, epithet, sarcasm, such as startled his provincial circle of readers, and directed all this at the Octopus, Mr. Huntington, who is made immortal in his shame.

The conviction grows that this political controversy formed one of the high moments of Bierce's life, that he reveled in every phase of it. He had found in himself the heroic note to which he had once vibrated in the Civil War. As he hurried to Washington or back to San Francisco, or lobbied, or thundered in the press, it was the strenuous life, the 'great life,' the American life, that he was leading. . . .

In old age, although as little *resigned* as ever, he seems to have achieved a certain tranquillity which was not inconsonant with a thorough-going nihilism. Genius, for him, was 'serenity, fortitude, reasonableness'; and he gains these qualities in a certain measure. We find him at last living at the quieter pace of a 'genial and severe master,' conducting a kind of secret university for his few devoted pupils, who, like him, adore literature above all else.

'I have ceased to be "discovered,"' he writes to a friend, 'but my notoriety as an *obscurian* may be said to be world-wide and everlasting.' This is good-humored. And we find the serene note again. If he is forgotten or ignored, it is nothing to resent or grieve over. The 'unappreciated genius,' in his view, never had a good case. 'Nobody compels us to make things that the world does not want. We merely choose to. . . . Wise poets write for one another.'

And so we find letter after letter which reveals this preoccupation of a master with the cult of letters. He exerts himself in teaching and advising his 'little group of gifted obscurians.' He directs their reading: the verses of Pope, the prose of Edmund Burke. He warns them against the tendency toward realism, against incorporating the 'reform spirit,' against solecisms, against slang. Howells was dreadful! Fourteen solecisms on a single page. Bierce, for his part, was possessed of a passion for purity. He fulminated from his mountains against the times, warning his satellites of the ways of socialism and democracy, which at heart he hated. 'The world does not wish to be helped. . . . We must study humanity as one does the suns. The Middle Ages were yesterday, Greece the day before. The individual man is nothing, as a single star is nothing.'

His knowledge is not the fruit of an organized labor, but it is courageous, and it flashes. And dipping long into his letters, informal in tone as they are, observing everywhere the immense effort and patience he expended upon initiates—who did not reward him, as it chanced, with works of genius—we note with surprise the entire absence of cynicism in *this* compartment of the man. It is perhaps ingenuous of me, but I am persuaded that Ambrose Bierce found his main happiness—'intermittent as that may have been'—more often and more protractedly in the cult of literature than in the society of women. Here was his good life, lived in his obscure corner, as he presided over his unknown school. It was a last unselfish hope—thwarted and disabused as he was in so many directions—that in his teachings he would eternalize himself. 'It is through you two,' he writes to his favorite pupils, 'that I expect my best fame.' [5]

[5] George Sterling and George Herman Scheffauer, who both committed suicide.

VI

AN ENEMY OF THE WEST: LAFCADIO HEARN

IN THE grim dull American past with its numberless documents of resigned spirits living out their sober days amid so much hard work, social conformity, and moral 'innocence,' it is in the highest degree exciting to encounter an occasional intransigent who resists, cries out, fights for his life. The spirit of romance was dead in the Gilded Age, but in Lafcadio Hearn we have a belated romanticist living for his natural emotions, pursuing always, in the face of everything, his scandalous, sensational existence.

The mere narration of Lafcadio Hearn's career, with its air of remoteness from everyday life, its constant invitation to picturesque passions, quixotic adventures, forms an interlude of bright fantasy in the monotonized period. In him there was a mingling of strange bloods that accounts perhaps for the aesthetic and exotic strain, a strain, in any case, which was typical of the enders-of-the-century almost everywhere. That he could survive for a space of years on the American continent was due largely to his remaining in the south with (for a time) its greater personal liberties, its more amiable conventions, persisting until the backward region was swung into the national rhythm. A man could survive then, though by his own confession knowing nothing at all about the things he ought to know, about a watch, a horse, a boat, a farm, about money; though living exclusively in the realm of his own hopes and his imagination. But there would be times when existence became too solitary, too futile, for the dreamy sensualist, and he would find himself the victim of his melancholy instability. His record thereafter would be a great pattern of flight—toward the blue Gulf, to the tropical islands, ultimately to the Far East.

He had arrived upon the pavement of Manhattan in 1869 among hordes of immigrants. He was nineteen. He was a runaway. The fact that he was of mixed race, Irish and Greek, that he had been separated from his parents in childhood and educated somewhat harshly in Jesuit schools, did not make him the happier. He had the infirmity, moreover, of a ruined eye injured in a school game, so that the remaining orb, myopic, swollen by much usage, rendered him to his own mind a repulsive figure. Shabby and unnaturally shy, Lafcadio Hearn passed two mysterious years in the gutters or even the cellars of New York, of which he would never speak again. He was morbid, defiant, without friends;

he was an outcast flung into the lowest depths of human society. One can only liken this obscure phase to the experiences of De Quincey in his darkest London years.

Under such forbidding conditions, and with little formal training, it was clearly through his abundant talent and disposition alone that Lafcadio Hearn became an artist, a worshiper of beauty—though of a rather exotic, macabre beauty, one would have said, flourishing by night in graveyards and morgues. His character of an exquisite in tattered garments, his eloquence in conversation, his marked 'temperament,' all these traits made him known to a small circle in Cincinnati, where he had come to work as a journalist. Certain grisly recitals of local murders had even brought him a modest notoriety. But the citizens of the transposed Puritan city found one day that Hearn worshiped beauty in the form of a mulatto woman who had befriended and sheltered him in his need, and after some time the resultant scandal prompted him to remove himself further.

Lafcadio Hearn, who had been abandoned by his parents, cast off by his guardian, oppressed by Jesuits, and starved by Americans, was by now quite undeceived by Christian civilization. He was, in fact, ripe for other faiths. In his boyhood, as he relates, he had once found with delight a book containing pictures of Greek sculpture; but his rigorous Irish mentor had torn out or marred the beautiful pages. And so Lafcadio, by childhood memories, had always associated physical beauty and harmony with the heathen races and had dreamed of them as forbidden things. The qualities of goodness and truth he encountered more often among the primitive and colored races.

It was in New Orleans that Hearn found himself happiest. He had wandered south in search of the tropical, the barbarous, of the blinding sun and heat which his passionate organism craved; and here moreover was a beautiful city which, more than any other in the new world, bore the evidence of a splendid past. A Spanish, a French, and then an Anglo-Saxon civilization had struggled in turn for possession of the southern seaport; and the old public buildings commemorated this historical fact. Even in 1877 the descendants of the Spanish and French colonists persisted in the old Creole quarter. To cross Canal Street into the Vieux Carré was simply to enter an old French city, where no English was spoken, where even the mulattoes and negroes spoke 'Ghombo,' the French patois of the Creoles.

'I am with Latins,' Hearn now wrote in an early letter to a friend in Cincinnati; 'I live in a Latin city. I eat and drink and converse with members of the detested race. I see beauty all around me—tropical, intoxicating. . . .' He found that something noble and brilliant, in the almost forgotten life of the dead south, still survived in New Orleans. 'Its atmosphere is European; its tastes are governed by European literature and the culture of the Old World.'

Installing himself in the heart of the old French quarter, he soon became absorbed in this new life, and as an artist sought to study 'its form and color and passion,' while living the irresponsible life of a bohemian. A lover and searcher of the folk-spirit, he found enough of the picturesque, enough poetry, legend, superstition, family pride, and all the 'splendid indolence and the splendid sins of the old social system.' As elsewhere, he shunned polite society and lived among pariahs, those who though poorest of all in worldly goods were rich in the primitive, exotic beauty which appealed most to him. For New Orleans was veritably a transplanted African capital, and Hearn was an early connoisseur of negro beauty and art. Much in advance of his time he tasted with joy the songs of the black people, their impassioned dances, the objects they made, the costumes they wore. And greatly alienated by the pretended Puritanism of his white contemporaries (which retained the hypocrisy but none of the spiritual intensity of the old Calvinists), Hearn felt a powerful call in those who bore the 'fine warm tints of tropical flesh.' He dreamed along the levee; he wandered down the many miles of quais, haunting the Caribbean sailing-ships and their polyglot crews. At night, in the yellow tropical moonlight, as he wrote tenderly, 'when the heavens seemed transformed into an infinite ocean of liquid turquoise,' he would listen to the long clarion calls of the boats in the harbor, visible from a great distance; or he would roam the segregated district of the Old City, where the harlots of many colors, who slumbered all day, now began to stir upon their balconies in all their finery.

His living-quarters, lined with esoteric books—for he was a scholar of the curious—was situated in the interior courtyard of an old mansion, reached by a huge archway, a hundred feet long, and full of reverberant echoes. Here there were palms and graceful banana trees, whose giant leaves split into bright ribbons; the great court was verdant with moss, and vines embraced the white pillars of the piazzas, climbing up and up the tinted walls. The great windows of his room looked across tropical gardens and magnificent half-ruined buildings. A fountain murmured faintly near by. . . .

He had an illusion of security and repose; he had the illusion of having escaped from unbeautiful conditions, intolerable pressures. The romanticist in his refuge meditates thus: 'Without, cotton-floats might rumble and street cars vulgarly jingle their bells; but these were mere echoes of the harsh outer world. Without, roared the Iron Age, the angry waves of American traffic; within one heard only the murmur of the languid fountain, the sound of deeply musical voices, conversing in the language of Paris and Madrid, the playful chatter of dark-haired children lisping in sweet and many-voweled Creole.'

Lafcadio Hearn, in short, was one of the rebels of art who multiplied in the closing years of the nineteenth century. Hating the cold north, he had found an 'island' for himself in New Orleans—one of the regions in America that resisted longest the harsh new influences. He could earn a living writing short pieces, odd sketches, even translations of his beloved Gautier and Nerval, for a press that was not yet yellow. He could live an unhampered life of his own among the tropical and somewhat sinister elements he preferred, and under their influence his talents for a romantic and musical prose could take an exotic and lonely growth.

Hearn scarcely impresses us at this time as an original thinker; he is rather an egoistic, almost an adolescent, one. It is with an air of deliberate eccentricity, of overcoming a quite marked sense of physical inferiority, that he seeks distinction by worshiping the 'Esoteric, the Odd, the Strange, the Queer, the Monstrous.' He announces himself a pagan, ruled by the Greek conception of 'beauty, nudity, fate.' Passion was the inspiring breath of Greek art, and the mother of language: its gratification, the act of a creator, and the divinest rite in Nature's Temple (*sic*). 'Virginity, Mysticism, Melancholy—three unknown words, three new maladies brought to us by the Christ. . . .' His Epicureanism is systematic: unless he can enjoy 'mad excesses,' he tells us, he cannot think, work, write; his mind remains arid and desolate!

It is interesting to note the dangers which Lafcadio ran in uttering at random, even in letters and newspaper sketches, such notions as belong rather to the post-Freudian era with its progressive dissolution of moral values. Everywhere at that time, social pressure, social contagion, stamped men with the same traits; youth was brought up on Miss Louisa Alcott and the *Rollo* books; at the worst it read the moderated Byronism of Thomas Aldrich, and was warned even by Howells against the brutal Zola. It was a time when a moral conformity of the utmost rigor and of an unruffled surface was strenuously imposed upon all men. The eccentricity of Hearn seems like a retort to the repressions and ostracisms he felt himself victim of. And in turn we expect him, as naturally occurred, to be isolated and condemned as a sort of moral plague-spot.

The dangers of a half-articulated dissent, of eccentricity almost for its own sake and subject to no discipline, no system of values which replaces the rejected one, are implicit in Lafcadio Hearn's career. He becomes a solitary, derided figure; he must conceal his mode of life, lie away his godless beliefs. His existence is unstable, torn between the need for limitless sensations and the need for order. He finds no medium in which he may express himself completely through a labor of patience and resolution. He is a lesser Swinburne with no band of Pre-Raphaelites to explain or defend him; and the French romantics or symbolists who might have welcomed or taught him are equally far away. All of his work is fragmentary, scattered, now inept, now touched with perfection. He wrote essays, sketches, critiques, fantasies, based on the folk-lore of Hindus, Chinese, Creoles, Africans, Japanese, and a great volume of letters which yield us the wavering line of his life. And so we have no single masterpiece, no Complete Works, but their torso: fragments that compose a character—a character of the sinful, rebellious type met with in older literatures—who flourishes secretly and stubbornly for a time in the inhospitable atmosphere of America's Gilded Age, and offers himself always in the ornate over-colored and rhythmic prose of the romantics whom he adores and emulates.

For all his disheveled life and his frequentations of voodoo-women and barbarous rites (which gained him a local ill repute), Hearn was a divided soul. During long reveries that came with recurrent attacks of yellow fever, he would observe that his hair 'is turning gray at thirty.' He longs to 'trample himself under foot,' in the interests of his literature; for he suffered over his literature, aware of its shortcomings and driven by a passion for perfection. He was equal to the discipline of rewriting pages and sentences numberless times in search of the desired rhythm and color. He would say, 'For me, words have color, form, character: they have faces, ports, manners, gesticulations: they have moods, humors, eccentricities—they have tints, tones, personalities. . . . Surely I have never yet made and never expect to make any money. Neither do I expect to write ever for the multitude. I write for beloved friends who can see color in words, can smell the perfume of syllables in blossom, can be shocked with the fine elfish electricity of words.'

It was a cult that Lafcadio Hearn practiced, all romantic and aesthetic. How, then, could he subsist, how cope with the world, how indeed carry on through the ignoble routine of journalism which 'dwarfs, stifles, emasculates, thought and style'? Though he had won some recognition for his charming sketches in the press, from a polite society more tolerant than that of the north, he had kept few friendships; he had preferred, in truth, his friends of the half-world and those of the Quadroon Ball. His special gifts, he presumed, were for evoking strange effects of color and image, as in *Chita;* and he had pursued only sensations which poisoned him. Besides, there were no literary circles in New Orleans, no jovial coteries, no cheering associates, save those vampire ones. . . . He hated the gas-light; he damned the American disposition to work people to death, and the American delight in being worked to death. After ten years he had exhausted New Orleans, which for that matter had become drastically altered. The new south would soon have no aristocracy, no lives of unbridled luxury, no mad pursuit of costliest pleasures, no reckless splendors of hospitality; the picturesque was vanishing before the approach of industrialism. The belated romanticist felt himself buried alive, or left to die in a city cursed with desolation like that of Sinbad the Sailor!

2

Years of exile now began for Lafcadio Hearn. He was departing in protest not only against American society; inarticulately his nature was opposed to the whole white man's civilization.

At first he went to live in the West Indies. All one's years might be delightfully dozed away in a land where the air is always warm, the sea always the color of sapphire, the woods perpetually green as the plumage of a parrot. 'Here the rude, warm savage Southern Nature succeeds in persuading you that labor and effort and purpose are foolish—that life is very sweet without them—the struggle for life in the North is madness.'

He resolved to stay in Martinique forever. For he had come to hate 'all that is energetic, swift, rapid . . . all competition, rivalry, all striving in the race for success,' in short, the whole democratic individualistic order of life with which he had failed to reconcile himself in the United States. Everything here was primitive and morally pure—'except in the only particular where purity would be out of harmony with natural conditions.' And so he could devote himself at last to that which he considered his forte: 'the study of tropical Nature—violent, splendid, nude and pure. . . .'

From the Windward Islands Lafcadio Hearn wrote back to civilization his romantic defense of the primitive world in *Two Years in the West Indies.* He foresaw a future for himself of penetrating farther and farther beyond the frontiers of white civilization; of adventuring, of exploring, in the jungles of South America, Africa, or the East. For when he returned to the United States and walked the stone streets of her cities the wanderlust possessed him. He was the creature of his nostalgias. One thinks of Baudelaire's outcry, 'Anywhere! Anywhere! out of the world!'

Lafcadio Hearn had found the utmost of that picturesque which he loved; he had found something that bathed his soul, among the fantastic populations who seemed to issue from the *Arabian Nights*, and who lived in green, lemon-yellow, and blue towns that were like ruined paradises of the seventeenth century. Here were men naked to the waist, very black or gold or bronze-skinned, who passed him noiselessly with barefoot strides. Here were women in the gay market-place, in brilliant-hued robes, with turbans of startling yellow. The air of the port was thick with the scents 'of sugar and cinnamon—with odors of mangoes and custard apples, of guava jelly and fresh cocoanut milk.'

And sometimes as he followed mountain roads toward the interior of the island, strange sounds would come rolling out of the forest—a weird alternation of pattering and booming, now sharp as a reverberation of distant volley firing, now an abysmal muttering. . . . 'It is the beating of an African drum, the tapping of a tamtam by fingers of iron. As you draw nearer the sense of a marvelous rhythm bursts upon you—a rhythm unlike anything you ever heard or imagined before. It brings to you a singular shock—the sudden knowledge that you have entered into a world not your own and that a soul is speaking in that savage rhythm, uttering syllables of a tongue which you do not know but which stirs something ghostly within you like a thought forgotten a million years. And at last when the full sound storms and bounds in beating eddies about you, . . . all your animal life struggles and throbs in response to that exultant barbaric measure. . . .'

Lafcadio lived for two terrible years in the Windward Islands. Prostrated by the tropical heat, his mind became like a garden whose rare flowers returned to their primitive forms, or were smothered by rank growths. If he revolted, attempted to energize his mind, to think, a subtle touch of fever would leave him helpless and senseless again for months. In the end, his friends aided him to return to the United States; and he came to New York with the hope of securing literary work. But New York was unthinkable; it could only be a 'jumping-off place' for new voyages.

W. C. Brownell, the accomplished young critic who had returned to New York in the late '80s after long absence, describes the stupefaction experienced in revisiting the young American metropolis. After the measured tones of Parisian life (so fruitfully compared in his *French Traits* with the different ones of American society), New York and America looming behind her were truly a vision of Carlyle's 'anarchy plus the constable.' Never before had the struggle for existence been more palpable, more naked, and more unpictorial. It would fare ill indeed with the dreamer or the *flaneur*, he reflects, once drawn into the mad currents that eddied about his omnibus.

For the *flaneur*, Lafcadio Hearn, returned from his monkeys and parrots, his violet skies and palms, New York was a cruel experience. He knew himself in 'the nerve-center of the world's activity,' in the most terribly organized of societies; but the effect upon him was of being pulled madly to right and left, of being 'caught in the beastly machinery and whirled in all directions,' until his senses were gone. He could find nothing; he could manage to see nobody. Everything seemed enigmatics and confusion. He expected momentarily to be struck dead as he wandered along the 'cubic miles of cut granite and iron fury,' as he faltered before an architecture and mechanics gone mad.

We may smile, wondering what poor Lafcadio would have made of our infinitely more elaborate organization, our Babylonian cosmopolis of 1930! Yet the city of the future existed already in 1889; the skyscrapers had begun to rear themselves above canyonlike streets. The elevated thundered ominously overhead. The bedlam of carts on cobbled pavements was but little removed from the anger of modern engines.

Lafcadio Hearn felt an unutterable weariness of the aggressive character of modern existence. He was less mad than the inhabitants. He saw their city with the imaginative eye of a half-sylvan primitive. Probably no other mind at the time, submerged, unidentified, anonymous as men became in the mass life, perceived the monstrous scale of things as did the poor Lafcadio.

Long afterward, an exile in the antipodes of the world, he would recall in an amazing vision the colossal modern city. In *Kokoro* he writes:

'The remembrance of a great city comes back to

me, a city walled up to the sky and roaring like the sea. The memory of that roar returns first; then the vision defines: a chasm which is a street, between mountains which are houses. I am tired, because I have walked many miles between those precipices of masonry and have trodden no earth—only slabs of rock—and have heard nothing but thunder of tumult. Deep below these huge pavements I know there is a cavernous world: systems underlying systems of ways contrived for water and steam and fire. . . . Above, the pale blue streak of sky is cut by a maze of spidery lines—an infinite cobweb of electric wires. Stairways of steel and cement, of brass and stone, with costliest balustrades, ascend through the decades and double-decades of stories; but no foot treads them. By water power, by steam, by electricity, men go up and down; the heights are too dizzy, the distances too great, for the use of limbs. . . . Orders are given and obeyed by machinery.

'And all this enormity is hard, grim, dumb; it is the enormity of mathematical power applied to utilitarian ends of solidity and durability. These leagues of palaces, warehouses, of business structures, of buildings describable and indescribable, are not beautiful but sinister. One feels depressed by the mere sensation of the enormous life which created them, life without sympathy; of their prodigious manifestations of power, power without pity. They are the architectural utterance of the new industrial age, and there is no halt in the thunder of wheels, in the storming of hoofs and of human feet. To ask a question, one must shout into the ear of the questioned. To see, to understand, to move in that high-pressure medium, needs experiences. The unaccustomed feel the sensation of being in a panic, in a tempest, in a cyclone. Yet all this is order.

'The monster streets leap rivers, span seaways with bridges of stone, bridges of steel. Far as the eye can read, a bewilderment of masts, a web-work of rigging, conceals the shores which are cliffs of masonry. Trees in a forest stand less thickly, branches in a forest mingle less closely, than the masts and spars of that immeasurable maze. Yet all is order.'

I have quoted at length from this passage because it unconsciously reaches a picturesqueness easily the equal of anything glimpsed in the West Indies. But it was of the essence of Hearn's romanticism to recoil from such a scene which literally cried for description—and surely a less lyrical description. He could compose nothing suitable of such monstrous materials. He must needs flee to a more favoring climate, where man had not effected so much sheer distortion of nature.

Lafcadio Hearn could not remain long in the great metropolis of the west. Irascible, shy, suspicious as a savage, he was little fitted for conventional, polite society. He outraged his friends; he insulted again and again the very editors who patronized him. It was all as if he were taking vengeance, half-consciously, for all the constraints and reproofs placed upon him.

He abhorred the fashionable literature of the day, the ubiquitous novels which happily ended at dutiful altars. There were so many ideas he had been forced to abandon, there were so many designs made abortive by the power of the censor! What outpourings he would have written, what transports of perfume and color and music! What did these tyros know of words? He felt himself at bay, an exile of art. He must again quit the civilized places. Every day spent in the turbulent world-city seemed more insane than the last.

'Carpets — pianos — windows — curtains — brass bands—churches! How I hate them! Would I had been born savage. The curse of civilized cities is upon me!'

He managed to conceal his rage from his colleagues for a few weeks, while he made preparations and acquired from the Harpers the commission for a voyage to Japan. Once disembarked in the magnificent harbor of Yokohama, he burnt his bridges, severed all his engagements and, penniless, unknown, flung himself upon the mercy of the Orient.

3

At first his romantic nature had been captured by this new adventure. Nothing later would ever surpass the excitement of the first impressions: here were Hokusai's own figures walking about in straw raincoats and straw sandals, bare-limbed peasants and patient-faced mothers; here were street-vistas of jinrickshas, of mushroom-shaped hats, queer elfish houses under blue roofs. It was as if he had dropped into the mediaeval world of a thousand years ago. Indeed, he had the feeling of having escaped from 'an almost unbearable atmospheric pressure into a rarefied medium.' The sense of a delightful confusion, seen through a flutter of flags and of drapery marked with Japanese or Chinese characters, persisted only for a short time, to be succeeded in the end by a conviction of arrangement and order. 'Gradually the eye begins to recognize in a vague way some general plan in the queerly gabled houses, the shops, the dresses of the laborers and merchants.' And beyond the edge of the town, during the visit to a Buddhist shrine, within sight of the mysterious snowy cone of Fujiyama, the sacred mountain, he had felt the influence of the Eastern faith for the first time.

But after his first breathless sorties along the harbor, his favorite frequentations with the great common people, peasants, fishermen, geisha girls, who represented for him the national virtues and the old customs—after his excursions into the interior to old villages, where he found all the local gods and legends unchanged—he felt the hand of an implacable order, such as he had rightly suspected, close upon him, holding him fast despite the outcries and wailings of his perennial waywardness. There was something of iron behind the gentle, smiling mask of this people.

He found employment at first as a teacher, then as professor of English literature at universities. He married—the daughter of a noble samurai, reduced by the industrial era—and was held by inconceivable ties of family, children, ancestors, retainers, such as he had never dreamed. The bohemian disappeared; and the professor who left each morning for his classroom passed out of his house before nine prostrate servants, as a great man. His work was hard; and Japan was grateful for his services, ultimately regarded as considerable and distinguished; but then, neither would she permit the object of her gratitude—strange friend and servitor—to remove himself at his whim. Once the novelty of the exotic land wore off, this man without a country, this romantic 'enemy of Western civilization,' saw himself caught, an exile for all eternity among a people who remained, at heart, forever strange. Too late, he made loud and bitter outcries of his deception and his grief. . . .

There is an immense pathos in the wanderings of Lafcadio Hearn to the ends of the earth. Although older Americans, like Henry James, Adams, and Brownell, longed, if not to live in Europe, at least to transplant the amenities of Europe to the United

States, he, the immigrant, could not have returned. He knew what he had fled from in England or France; he had departed in search of a new chance, new fortune. Moreover his whole intellectual or sensuous education had taken place in the United States. But the trial had ended in failure after twenty years: America had only represented the traits of Western Europe, intensified, naked, unmitigated by humanism.

At this time Hearn, like so many of his generation, had been strongly influenced by the reading of Spencer's *First Principles* and *Data of Ethics.* At forty he was no longer the neurotic, irresponsible bohemian. He had been interested from the first, through his studies in folk-lore, in the forms of human society and the evolution of customs, and this had led him, with troubled mind, to question Western civilization in all its aspects. Where others had complacently accepted the elevated railway or the underground as monuments to human intelligence, he had preferred the 'backwardness' of tropical peoples. And now, in Spencer's attempt at synthesis, he had found a certain inspiration; he had accepted the Victorian belief in the unity of nature and in an orderly progression of phenomena. Where others turned pessimist at the indifferentism of nature, he had acquired a new reverence for all forms of faith and all the arts of life. He came to the East with a mind prepared to accept its values and to be its spokesman.

The highest drama of expatriation, in form and degree far more intense than anything hitherto seen, is contained in his many letters, written from Japan during a period of fifteen years. For us who now question the direction and value not only of American society, but—in renewed skepticism—of the whole Western culture, the reflections of Hearn are surprisingly valid. He was an early prophet of the rising Orient, whose career the whole Western world had begun to watch and whose impact upon the West is now so strongly felt. But even more valuable was the double perspective which Hearn gained: he could at once view with splendid detachment the mechanized life of America, and he could observe (with a sinking heart) the same system close at hand, in the process of conquering Japan and changing the mediaeval nation into an industrial power of the Western order.

The whole suggestion of the old Japanese form of life, as he saw it through long residence and travel in the unspoilt interior of the island, was of a harmonious, *natural* society created by its racial traditions and its religion. This had resulted in the complex human arts, the elaborate etiquette which governed every phase of life, even to the pretty words and smiles whose exact expression or duration were prescribed by an ancient discipline. In America, of course—to which old Japan offered a supreme, illuminating contrast—he had seen no code of manners, no veritable rule of life, that resulted in an embellished human relationship, in a healthy and honest society. And what was most important here was that the sense of beauty, sprung from the good life, the natural life, had become a living force: it was felt in the exquisitely cared-for gardens, in the admirable, delicate objects of daily use, the images of infinite hand-made variety produced by peasants and artisans; it was alive in the souls of the natives who opposed the use of their pretty waterfalls for hydroelectric power! As he lingered over the things they made, over the sculptures of animals, or the phallic images seen at Shinto shrines, Lafcadio Hearn divined the simple, truthful beauty of the primitive impulse in art—perhaps a generation before the primitive was to become an absolute vogue. He became as sure as he was of death that Japan was far in advance of the West in its feeling for art; that a print of Hokusai or those who came after him was worth more than all the fabulous canvases that crowded our lifeless museums! The sense of beauty functioned simply as part of the domestic life, the ritual, the customs of the people. There was great art in the adornment of a lady's hair, in the design of her comb, and in the folk-dances, as surely as there was in the carven Buddha of the temple. And underneath the mysterious web of myth, superstition, and magic, he felt 'the soul of the race,' uniting, vivifying, governing all; the ancient religion, the old communal ways, were as hierarchical, as predetermined and just, as the life-system of the ants.

As an American Lafcadio Hearn had cried out again and again that he lacked the greed, the 'aggressive cunning,' requisite to survive, or to retain the advantages which his merit might win. Here an age-old communism had worked upon the people since the very inception of their civilization. A coercion, sanctified by ancient customs, operated upon the individual in a hundred different ways, suppressing competition as it was known in the West.

One day he had engaged a jinricksha man, a strong young fellow who had sprung swiftly away at top speed; but upon overtaking a feeble old runner, the younger man had dropped behind and slackened his pace to a walk instead of bounding by. Appeals were of no avail. The unwritten law for all workers in Japan held that 'you must not try, without special authorization, to pass your fellows.'

Truly, old Japan was a world upside-down. But the Oriental had learned to make his peace with life and eternity; and his religion, while setting terrible limits, outwardly, enriched all his inner life. Nirvana, light, came, according to Buddhism, with the destruction of consciousness. Once the illusion of Mind, of that which we call the Self, was destroyed, 'Reality was revealed as infinite vision and infinite peace.'

What was ancestor-worship—so ill understood by Occidentals—but the subjection of individual appetites to the will of the numberless ghosts or spirits who abounded everywhere, to the force of the past and the race-will?

Lafcadio Hearn declared himself a Buddhist. Once more he abjured Christianity and made vehement attacks upon the missionaries, to the surprise of cultivated natives long accustomed to go, as 'heathens,' undefended. The missionaries were unconscious destroyers, he wrote in the Japanese press; they were the arm of penetration of Western capitalism; they would bring the red-brick factory and the counting-house which were the symbols of modern Christianity!

In a letter to an American friend Hearn now called himself 'pariah and renegade,' pointed out everywhere as an infidel in the eyes of white men, and lost to all decency and shame. But he would risk all to resist Progress a little.

'There will be no conversion to Christianity,' he exclaims. '*I hope to see a United Orient yet, bound in one strong alliance against our cruel Western civilization.* If I have been able to do nothing else in my life, I have been able to oppose a little . . . that which is called civilization.'

Lafcadio Hearn had become an enemy of the West. Amazing revolt against a whole system of life! He was transfigured in his pride and solitude and dared oppose all alone the cycle of industrial progress in the East. He writes now with a beautiful anger of the changes in America, which he scans keenly from far-off Matsue. Henceforth, his letters from month to month furnish an extraordinary review of American life, a treasury of comment, criticism, and prophecy.

The Oriental adventure has been revealing, educational. 'How it opens a man's eyes and mind,' he would say, 'about his own country, about conventionalisms, false ideals and idealisms, of a hundred sorts.' His contempt for the business class of northern mankind has become an obsession. The tyranny of the future as he saw it in 1893 must be that of the monopoly, the trust, the coldly mathematical combination—infinitely less human than robber-barons such as Charlemagne or Barbarossa. Like Henry Adams, who mused before the dynamo of the Chicago Exposition, Hearn too foresaw the weak human pawns enslaved to 'the colossal dynamo, exact and dangerous and powerful.' Monopolies would continue to grow, to coalesce, and eventually contain all. The state itself would become one monstrous trust. Life would be regulated to infinitesimal detail, as in factories and railroads. For men were learning already to live 'within the eight-day clock of modern life.' Love, honor, idealisms, were no longer absorbing motives; the primary materials were being replaced under the more complex conditions by the 'substitutes' of modern manufacture. The rule of the many would be 'as merciful as a calculating machine, and as moral as a lawn mower.'

'As surely as human nature is not perfect will the directing class eventually exploit the wonderful situation—as Roman rulers exploited the world. . . . When the fighting and competition among the Barons has ceased, a "democracy" more brutal than any Spartan oligarchy will control all life. The future tyranny will be worse than of old—for it will be a régime of moral rather than physical pain, and there will be no refuge from it.'

'And even the power to flee away,' he resumes in these letters of the '90s whose rare prescience we marvel at, 'out of the land, to dwell among beasts and birds, might be denied!'

What would become of the humanities, he wondered? Literature in America was being written chiefly by women; while the best of American authors, such as Henry James, he commented, were exiles like himself, in London or Paris or Florence. But then, where were even those liberties he recalled from the period of 1870? A man could no longer print his thoughts in any periodical of influence. And with a splendid divination of the course of mass life and the necessary standardization of taste he foretold that in a generation, 'publishers' syndicates will decide what the public shall be allowed to read. . . . A man will write only what he is told to write.'

One might say that Hearn, in the fragments of his brilliant letters, summed up almost every aspect of the dilemma in which artists like Whistler, Melville, Henry James, or Bierce, all fugitives or solitaries, had found themselves.

'*We little, petty outsiders—gnats hovering about life!*' he exclaims. '*There isn't any more room for us!* The world is become methodical as an abacus. . . . One thing is sure: in another generation there can be no living by dreaming of art.'

4

Hearn's apostasy and flight from the United States had been undertaken no doubt with some basic hopes of finding 'the good life,' or at least the climate and environment in which his temperament could thrive. Among the peasants of the interior of Japan, with their lovely old folkways and their genius for crafts, he had hoped for a strong stimulus to fertile production. But now he was fated to see the old Japanese life, with the special amenities and restraints which he had celebrated, passing away before his eyes. Heeding his admonitions no more than those of Herbert Spencer, Japan wedded herself to the Western economy; while the factories, the slum-quarters of Manchester and Pittsburgh, the grimy docks of London and New York, were duplicated with an added touch of horror. The passing of the household religion and all gentle usage was not at once followed by the adoption of Western discipline, so that the charming peasants and artisans of Japan sank, demoralized, under the most brutal exploitation. Poor Lafcadio could witness the whole process from close by. He could see the sewing-machine shop installed every day next to the image-maker's shop.

In fleeing to the antipodes of the world the bohemian had neither left behind nor evaded the civilization which he cursed. The age turned a deaf ear to all libertarians. There was a fatality in this; and the comedy enacted itself everywhere. The Japanese listened no more to Hearn than the New England mill-owners had listened to Thoreau.

The author of *Chinese Ghosts* and *Chita* dragged out his life in the great cities of Japan, his talents for romantic prose being largely diverted by the labors of a professor of literature. In various ways he bore the familiar Calvary of the expatriate. More than Henry Adams, who had felt himself snubbed and patronized by literary Europe, and Henry James, who suffered the loneliness of the true cosmopolitan, Hearn felt himself tragically uprooted.

It is the fate of the true cosmopolitan, the eternal foreigner, to stand always in factitious and artificial relationship with the society in which he finds himself. The part he plays in the life about him can seldom be a great or happy one. Thanks to his anomalous position among the nations, he is assailed by divers special diseases and anxieties.

Lafcadio Hearn mourned: 'Every day it strikes me more and more how little I shall ever know the Japanese. Sympathy and friendship are almost impossible to obtain. . . .'

In spite of everything, he was a stranger, he declared, to his wife, who emanated nevertheless all the formal sweetness and submission of the Japanese woman. But under the mask of regulated smiles and courtesies on the part of children, servants, relatives, pupils, how thin was the disciplined emotion! Never the joy and pain, the passion and forgiveness, of Western or Latin natures. Never a *frisson*, a thrill, across the fatal division of the hereditary types! And there was the harder side of Japanese character, a certain 'far-offness' about friends even when they killed themselves to please you, an absence of familiarities, a silent strength, a firmness of steel, a nobility without tenderness, without 'that immense reserve force of love and forgiving power which even the rougher men of the West have.'

In the end, it is clear that Hearn was intensely unhappy in Japan. Sensitive to the verge of paranoia, he became convinced of Japanese ingratitude. 'After having worked during thirteen years for Japan,' he wrote in 1903, 'and sacrificed everything for the Japanese, I have only been driven out of the service and practically banished from the country.'

He dreamed now of returning for a visit to the United States—difficult as it was to separate himself from his family—as a lecturer in one of her great universities. He would have liked to see the deeply changed land in which he had suffered and exulted so blindly. From far off he imagined in his visions her colossal new machinery, her teeming populations, her prodigious material efforts. He perceived, as he phrased it in his last letters, a growing feeling of 'human brotherhood' under the rough exterior; he foresaw a happier condition once the era of cruel competition had ended. And the artist might after all survive in a new rôle; he would still pursue the beauty that is all about us, 'that travels on railroads and lodges at hotels . . .' fighting against ugliness, apathy, selfishness! Lafcadio Hearn's aesthetic was more dignified now, but none the less romantic. He saw, at length, artistic opportunities of great scope in the high-pressure civilization, and he is very suggestive on this score: 'Its monstrosities and glooms and tragedies infernal, give opportunity for the grandest contrasts ever made!'

It was too late. The domestic bonds of this Japanese citizen were very heavy. When he would have gone to America the Imperial Government detained him; and when at length it freed him, the invitation from the United States had been withdrawn. During the bad days of the Russo-Japanese War, Lafcadio Hearn died suddenly at the age of fifty-four.

His later books, such as *Glimpses of Unfamiliar Japan*, *Out of the East*, *Japanese Fairy Tales*, and *Kokoro*, which painted an exotic world with great sensitiveness and with a rare sympathy, had gathered a certain fame. The imaginative writings, including tales, fantasies, and ghost stories based on folk-lore, were quietly enjoyed by the aesthetic '90s; for us they have 'dated,' and we must taste their fragile charms in despite of an over-cloying sweetness and a prevailing lyricism. *Japan: An Interpretation*, which Hearn completed before his death, is more reasoned, more complete, than his previous essays in Oriental civilization, and retains after a quarter of a century the deepest interest for those who would compare our own forms of life with those of the East.

Lafcadio Hearn was a minor artist; he contributed no invention, no energizing principle of form, that could give his work a significant order and force. None knew this better than he, or contended more with his own limitations. But then, the painful upheavals of his life, the persecutions which we have noted, the silence of contemporaries, the absence of suitable examples, the pressure of grinding poverty, all combine mockingly to make a dark enough record of adverse conditions to explain the dispersed, the abortive, career.

The talent of the Gilded Age was moderate. There

were few geniuses; but then perhaps we make no more such. Yet large or small as the talent might be, the rate of sheer destruction or export of this vital commodity, attained at this period by the happy republic, seems something appalling and uncalculated.

VII

THE VOYAGE OF STEPHEN CRANE

Brise ton crucifix, sème au vent les atomes
De l'Idéal futile et suis la tourbe lente;
Car nous ne savons pas même ce que nous sommes.
—FRANCIS VIELÉ-GRIFFIN.

MOST of us can remember the somewhat 'Biedermeier' atmosphere of our youth and childhood in the small town or suburb of thirty to forty years ago. We remember the green and red stuffed furniture of those days, the marble-topped tables, the heavy draperies and consequently musty rooms, the scroll-work exteriors of the Reign of Terror in architecture, the black carriages in Sunday promenades. All the casual, undiscriminating surface of American life, that we may recall visually, composes a *style* that persisted from the Civil War approximately to the World War, from the age of the railroad to that of the motor car. The letters and memoirs and the yellowed periodicals of this ugly half-century bear out our impressions of the unconscious and inarticulate, if animated, period now viewed coldly from the perspective of a whole generation. If we would elicit a moral out of the zero level of literary and artistic output resulting from, accompanying, all the throb and effort, the animated and absorbing mass rhythms, it would be that life *was*, at its best and essentially, unconscious and inarticulate.[1] Historians who groped toward some human scheme of things, who approached universal questions candidly and tried to calculate the immediate future, lived and slept wanly beside the great void which they glimpsed. They could make nothing credible out of the contemporary throng that rushed by on interminable errands or appetites and that suggested, as Henry Adams said, the attitude of deep-sea fish toward the elements in which they swam.

The Americans were only surprised by death; and Europeans said of them that they tended toward violent and sudden deaths in great measure. But neither by the embellishment of their daily lives nor by the discipline of meditation was death prepared for. This surprise at the preposterous intrusion of death, in the form of a banal crisis, is often and aptly voiced by the typically American Stephen Crane. Death evokes surprise and anger, since American life is so profoundly irreligious. To Crane it occurs often that 'nature does not regard him as important, and that she feels she would not maim the universe by disposing of him.' And so he at first

[1] The generation born between 1860 and 1870 produced one brilliant *prosateur,* who threatened to become a genius but died early in Europe; several literary exiles; two famous *French* poets (Merrill and Vielé-Griffin); a few imitative painters and neurotics.

wishes to throw bricks at the temple, 'and he hates deeply the fact that there are no bricks and no temple.'

In the 1880s Stephen Crane grew up in one of the small towns lying near the groaning agglomeration of New York. He played baseball and dreamed of excelling as a professional hero. Everywhere about him in New Jersey there were the scattered hills, the lots filled with rubble and rusting tin, composing a severe landscape—so changed from that of Thoreau in New England, or of Henry James in Albany—in which youth was passed. Crane idled by the seashore, growing in the sun. Circuses wandered by and he could gape at merry-go-rounds, at animal trainers, theatrical cowboys, and sad Indians. Wild West stories were devoured in their turn, and boys and girls with daubed faces pranced about bonfires in the prosaic twilight of backyards. Trivial legends flourished everywhere, of frontiersmen who massacred North Americans, of bandits who derailed locomotives, of heroes who rose from canal boy or messenger boy to president or railroad president.

At a very early stage, however, an important hiatus appears between Crane's vision of life and the principles of his native society. Though he was the son of a minister he appeared to lose all faith in a just Providence; and while clinging, perhaps, to the human example of Christ, he grew hopeless of finding Christian principles anywhere applied. His dislike of Little Lord Fauntleroy costumes in childhood, of Tennyson's poems in boyhood, according to Mr. Thomas Beer, foreshadowed the 'bad boy' of American literature. And there is an early episode, retold by Crane's whimsical biographer, which strikes us as one of the high moments.

Playing one day near the ground of a circus, Stephen Crane picked up the hat of an Italian passing by, and received from him by way of reward a drink from a red bottle. (Stephen was only fourteen then.) In an ecstasy now, the boy returned home to his mother and minded not in the least going to the scheduled prayer-meeting with her. He appeared, in fact, quite soulful, and his emotion was construed as a sudden access of religious zeal. Whereas, it is apparent from now on, as he sulks or indulges in cynical outbursts, that a secret disaffection, a sense of moral disparities, had begun to grow in him early, and would be fortified with age. This in itself becomes the key to his personality.

With his gift of clairvoyance he would discern always the true motives of men; his extraordinary eyes plunged through protestations and subterfuges. Unable to live within subterfuge himself, he would suffer greatly for his good vision; he would be vexed by the need of explaining himself; he would dismiss accusations with evasive words. Others might look with Howells toward 'the more smiling aspects,' but

Crane would be intrigued by all the 'types' and scenes which belied these.

The prodigy of Syracuse College, and her gifted third-baseman, descended upon New York now as a free lance journalist; and soon he delighted in haunting the Bowery with its swarming of crude life, so appealingly close to the presses of Park Row. Under the green gas-lights, under the ominously rumbling elevated, derelicts reeled by him, saloons offered their stench of beer; the air of tragic side-streets was foul with refuse and the oaths of street-walkers. He would sleep for a night with mendicants in the lodgings of outcasts. One has no precise evidence of what echoes of French naturalism or Russian melancholy floated to the young Crane in 1890. But nothing could have drawn him to the purlieus of culture at this time; only his deep draughts of raw life delighted him.

His opportunities were great, and in certain ways he exploited them well. He translates his sensations with a vigor that is uncommon in American letters. 'All through the room,' he writes of one of his night lodgings, 'could be seen the tawny hues of naked flesh, limbs thrust into the darkness, projecting beyond the cots; upreared knees, arms hanging long and thin over the cot edges . . . statuesque, carven, dead.' It was his *Experiment in Misery*, born of his passion to see, to experience life directly; and he absorbed with his insatiable eyes impressions that he had learned to paint with a surprising power of evocation.

Refractory beliefs possessed him as he emerged from the degraded asylum of the East Side, to which he could imagine himself condemned. He glimpsed the multitude of buildings southward, of pitiless hue and sternly high, and they became 'emblematic of a nation forcing its regal head into the clouds, throwing no downward glances; in the sublimity of its aspirations ignoring the wretches who may flounder at its feet.' The roar of the city in his ear was to him the confusion of strange tongues, babbling heedlessly; it was the clink of coin, the voice of the city's hopes, which were to him no hopes.

'He confessed himself an outcast, and his eyes from under the lowered rim of his hat began to glance guiltily, wearing the criminal expression that comes with certain convictions.'

Stephen Crane's convictions may have been rebellious, but his eyes never 'glanced guiltily.' With much boldness he wrote his first novel, *Maggie: A Girl of the Streets*. This simple history of a seduction and desertion was an offering of immature genius; there was a charm, to be sure, in its clear, impersonal narration, an energy in its Hogarthian portraits that outweighed the neologisms and errors of syntax of a youth of twenty. Crane could have known of Goncourt and Zola, at this time, only in theory. He contributed, moreover, an 'impressionistic' style which secured vividness through the use of striking and well-placed detail.

A thorough-going skepticism, an instinctive artistic integrity, prevented Stephen Crane from moralizing; and though his methods were derived from the air of the times—abroad—from the restrained advocation by Howells and Henry James of the French masters, the young writer became the forerunner of the twentieth century realistic movements. He continued, in *The Red Badge of Courage*, to treat another social phenomena—war and military glory—with the same skepticism, the same mistrust. This masterpiece of a precocious youth of twenty-four was the painstaking, psychological portrait of a coward, in lieu of the proverbial celebration of violent heroism. Appearing at almost the same time as Zola's *La Débâcle*, to which it was likened, while smaller in scale and more intensely imaginative than the work of the French pacifist, *The Red Badge* became an affair of great novelty and busy polemics, a great contemporary success.

2

The most appealing quality of the young novelist was surely his experimental spirit. Thanks to his environment, his local traditions, and his sensitive reactions to physical adventure, he longed to experiment with danger. In this connection Mr. Beer suggests that his preoccupation with fear shows him an instinctive coward. It is more likely, however, in view of the premonitions that come to persons of tubercular predisposition, that he was morbidly interested in death as a theme which lent significance to life, which gave it form and style, whereas to most Americans death was ludicrous, indecent, unprepared for, the single mocking comment of the universe on their distracted, automatic lives.

Now as something of a philosopher, now as an adventurer, Stephen Crane proceeded to indulge his taste for travel and for a wealth of sensations. A young celebrity, with ample funds at his command, and the object of so much curiosity and gossip, he must live hard, extravagantly or violently. Like Ambrose Bierce and Mark Twain, he pushed toward the frontiers, the realms of Deadeye Dick and Buffalo Bill, who were the apostles of his boyhood. We are told that he loved to play with revolvers and that he sought danger willfully. He has narrow escapes from bandits in Mexico; he filibusters from Florida to Cuba so that he may taste revolution. He wanders over the western prairies, or rushes among the first to scenes of war. It was as if the scent of bloodshed and the closeness of death compensated for the uniform qualities, the want of interesting relief, which the more civilized American regions offered. It was as if no strong moral experience or convictions could be drawn from any events here short of cataclysm.

Only in the cruel transitions from the security and boredom of peaceful effort to disaster did he find stimulus.

When one thinks of the mild habits which European artists generally exhibit in their youth and of their colorless years of discipline ('chained to a table'), the spectacular, adventurous youth of Americans such as Melville and Poe, Bierce and Crane, assumes all the greater meaning. The Europeans lived vicariously for the most part, and in their ideas or their art found their highest adventure. As for the Americans, unless they clung to safety lines they were caught up and swept away by the undertow of violence which lurked always in the currents they floated on.

The playboy in Stephen Crane would be sobered and moved by catastrophes; he would find certainty again in his conviction of the injustice and senselessness of his universe.

In the famous filibustering episode in which he sailed out of Jacksonville on a tramp steamer loaded with arms for Cuba, Crane all but perished in shipwreck. For a day and a night he was adrift with a few comrades, and the story of this adventure, *In the Open Boat*, is one of his perfect things. It gives the exceptional, the tragic, experience without effort, with an engaging under-emphasis.

The night hangs interminably while the weary rowers await the issue. 'It was probably splendid,' he says. With the dawn, the color of the sea changes slowly 'from slate to emerald-green, streaked with amber lights. . . .' And when they are at last tumbled by great waves into the surf and go swimming through the tide toward shore, he catches sight of the bobbing water-jug which dances after their rout in the free play of the sea. But all through the night as they watched the lights of the land which was unaware of their fearful effort and their vigil, Stephen Crane had felt himself facing eternity with his habitual wonder and resentment. This mood serves as the refrain: 'If I am going to be drowned—if I am going to be drowned—if I am going to be drowned, why, in the name of the seven mad gods who rule the sea, was I allowed to come thus far and contemplate sand and trees? Was I brought here merely to have my nose dragged away as I was about to nibble the sacred cheese of life?'

The bitter accents, the absorption in death, may be found in nearly all his work. The story of *The Blue Hotel*, for instance, is admirable for its steady working up of a group of people in a small Nebraska hotel to the inevitable fight in which a hysterical Swede is stabbed by a little gambler. Nobody had intended to harm him, as he so persistently feared, from the outset; but at any rate there he is, a disagreeable corpse, lying alone on the floor of the saloon, with 'its eyes fixed upon a dreadful legend that dwelt atop the cash-machine: "*This registers the amount of your purchase.*" ' The killer, in the words of one of the characters, was only a kind of 'qualifying adverb'; all who had received or spoken to the Swede during the day of blizzard had been unknowingly collaborators of his death. '. . . That fool of an unfortunate gambler came merely as a culmination, the apex of a human movement.'

Another aspect of the young novelist's thirst for experiment was his frank incredulousness about so much social convention that passed unchallenged. With his abandonment of religion his belief in a public Puritanism of morals had certainly foundered, although he himself may have been privately Puritan. He may even have had some hankering curiosity to test Christian principles. . . .

He had been warned not to write another *Maggie;* this first novel, which had won him the friendly interest of Hamlin Garland and Howells, had never had more than an 'underground' edition. And when we recall how in those days no voice lifted itself among the drearily pious to question the moral customs of the Gilded Age, we understand all the better Joseph Conrad's observation that his friend Crane may have lacked 'circumspection' in his personal conduct.

During the several bohemian years in which he frequented the cafés and night restaurants of Broadway, the author of *Maggie: A Girl of the Streets* clearly exhibits a want of caution which we can only admire. His mistakes assume the character of a sort of lonely and gallant protest. He defends, for instance, a prostitute against a policeman who is beating her, and is himself beaten and thrown into jail. On another occasion he saves a street-woman in a quarrel with her pander, only to see her arrested by an arriving policeman for 'profanity.' (This incident has a cosmic humor which establishes its truth.) He even gives money to a 'fallen woman' on her professed plea that she means to 'reform,' and in the end she returns to blackmail him. Stephen Crane's letters are full of wisdom and humor during these bachelor years. He showed a frank interest in the half-world of New York, which seems tremendously interesting and yet neglected, as a reservoir of human experience. And what must have been most instructive of all in the end was the series of painful scrapes into which Crane's experiments led him.

'In March of 1896,' writes Thomas Beer, 'Crane seems to have been conscious that he was under fire.' At the outset of his success ugly scandals were set afloat, even reaching England, where he was regarded as Edgar Poe *redivivus!* Stephen Crane must be drunk to write such and such story; he must be stupefied with morphine! *Maggie* was a true story of his own villainous seductions, and the poor victim was even produced as evidence! Tales of his moral 'crimes' leaked out in the yellow press. The amount of sheer slander and envy which followed him would have been depressing if at the age of twenty-five Stephen Crane were really susceptible of disillusionment. By looking very closely at life it had come to appear a more terrible confusion than one had ever suspected; and by 'calling a spade a spade' occasionally he had simply made things worse for everybody.

In retrospect it becomes clear to us, despite the truncated, abortive output Stephen Crane has left, that aside from Henry James and Bierce he was the most naturally gifted writer of prose who had appeared in the second half of the century. Certainly his sense for language was a more spontaneous thing than either of these men possessed. But his immaturity was patent; and one awaited with suspense the completed knowledge in him both of the world and of his own faculties, so that he might arrive at more comprehensive, more ambitious designs.

But the conditions of American life seemed to penalize any marked originality in individuals. His intellectual independence had already done much harm to Crane's reputation. Though many were convinced of genius in him, he was given little assurance that his 'unpleasant' literature would receive aid. He must have been the recipient of much practical advice as to how to 'tone down' his stories, or divert his talents; and one can think of nothing more baffling than such advice to an impetuous artist. Nor could the intimacy of such literary personages as Richard

Harding Davis and Hamlin Garland—or even of James Huneker, for that matter—have been enough to stimulate him, or offer any critical intelligence equal to his own striking powers, his own interest in sheer craftsmanship.

However, I do not think that Stephen Crane was too conscious of all the pressure, the resistance, the contagion, and the felt omissions in American life, beyond the sense of a vague irksomeness. In his spirited way he rather enjoyed and preferred the American scene, which was at once so tempting and so disastrous to play with. To put some distance between himself and the tumultuous scene may have occurred to him as a means of simply improving both education and perspective. At any rate he was glad to leave the country when a great newspaper offered to send him to Greece, which had a real war in prospect for him. To be sure, nothing of savage Turks or routed Greeks could evoke again the eloquence of the wholly imaginary *Red Badge*. But in his voyages to and fro, between wars and love affairs in Greece or Cuba, he had discovered England, or rather London, where life seemed eminently possible on more favorable terms; and London had discovered him.

3

At this time an interesting group of artistic expatriates lived, joyed, or suffered, in various parts of England and the European continent. Henry James, who lived at the town of Rye, in Sussex, was perhaps the most accomplished of these exiles. But the roll of those Americans who found it more expedient to quit the country numbered, among many others, Bret Harte, living out his days in Scotland; James Whistler in London or Paris or Italy; F. Marion Crawford in Italy; Harold Frederic, author of a promising first novel, *The Damnation of Theron Ware,* in London; Henry Harland, editor of the famous *Yellow Book,* in London. Henry Adams too was in London with the American ambassador, John Hay, although his permanent home was in Paris now. And in Paris two gifted men, Stuart Merrill and Francis Vielé-Griffin, born in Long Island and Virginia, respectively, played an important part in the Symbolist movement, a notable revival of the art of poetry in France. Of these two, at least Merrill had made a conscious, long-pondered choice. He had abandoned his law office in New York, and taking his precious porcelains, vases, *objets d'art* with him, in 1891, had gone to the Left Bank of Paris, which had called him ever since his student days at the Lycée Condorcet.

Howells had written to him pleadingly: '. . . B. tells me that you are going abroad. I want you to be an American poet, and to write in English, or, if you must write first in French, to reinstate yourself afterward. A man is not born in his native country for nothing. I wish I might persuade you. . . .'

On the eve of the Spanish-American War, the United States had reached a peak of prosperity as the result of nearly two generations of industrial expansion. An incalculable wealth of gold had been amassed on the western side of the Atlantic. But on the eastern shores, the greater part of her artistic talent had gathered and added their definite contribution—James and Crane in England, Merrill and Vielé-Griffin in France—to the aesthetic life of the countries whose guests they were.[2]

An exciting literary movement in England had but recently died a melancholy death. The *Yellow Book* had been an Irish-Franco-American-English affair, in which the later stories of Henry James, such as *The Death of the Lion*, so vibrant with the literary life intensely lived, achieved as great fame in reality as the more obvious contributions of Beardsley and Wilde. The exotic magazine had come to grief, as sadly as its votaries. Wilde had been tried; Hubert Crackanthrope was drowned in the Seine; Beardsley died of consumption. And the Americans, Harland and Harold Frederic, wandered pathetically about London or Paris. Of the unfortunate

[2] Mrs. Deland, Mrs. Foote, Mrs. Freeman, Mrs. Burnham, Dr. S. Weir Mitchell, Mark Twain, William Dean Howells, Hamlin Garland, Frank R. Stockton, James Whitcomb Riley, and Thomas Bailey Aldrich, were among the more prominent of those who stayed in the United States.

Harland, who had tried to lead such a devoted, such an uncompromising, movement, James said, 'One would like to help him—and I try to—in talk; but he is not too helpable, for there is a chasm too deep to bridge, I fear, in the pitfall of his literary longings unaccompanied by the *faculty*.' Frederic had vowed never to return to the United States; an embittered man and a lover of alcohol, the literary faculty in him, too, seemed to dwindle until it had the guise only of a foreign correspondent's proficiency.

As for Henry James, he had undergone a sort of second birth in the favoring air of aestheticism, of renewed interest in form, exact language, and continental models. He had become the object of an admiring cult, and the only literary life to be had in England during the last years of the century, as Mr. Ford Madox Ford relates, was to live in the country and take tea with Mr. James.

This ill-assorted group of literary exiles (who often hated each other) and their English colleagues welcomed Stephen Crane. His celebrity had preceded him in England, where Mr. Edward Garnett had called him 'the chief impressionist of the age . . . the creator of fresh rhythms and phrases.' And Henry James, to whom Howells had warmly commended the young novelist, had also sung his praises.

The English were diverted by this defiant and tense little man with brilliant eyes, whose vocabulary suggested the man of action of dime drama, and whom Mr. Ford pretends to have often seen sitting about in breeches, leggings, and shirt sleeves, toying with a huge Colt revolver strapped to his belt. And Stephen Crane, who had, at present, a wife, Cora, appreciated the amenities of English life which permitted him to play now the unruly bohemian and now the great gentleman living in a 'style' which might bring about his arrest in New York.[3]

Although Stephen Crane had no conscious quarrel with his native land and differed sharply with other exiles in his defiant Americanisms, he found, after all, much that was stimulating and curious in the more brilliant world of London. The memory and the example of the great dead Victorians, of Arnold and Browning, of Swinburne and Stevenson, was still fresh. Moreover, the company of young writers such as Conrad and Wells and Ford amused him; and he found that he could profitably sit at the feet of the 'Old Man,' as he called Henry James. Crane himself had much to communicate; he had a method, a style, which broke with Anglo-Saxon tradition. The power of words was infernal in him; they must work like machines in the sentence, he would declare. And he exclaimed once, of Stevenson, to Ford Madox

[3] Was Cora really Stephen Crane's wife? Or was she an amazing Phryne of the American South? The silence of the conventionally loyal Crane family has left the record dark; but documents and letters recently discovered among the possessions of the late 'Cora Crane,' and as yet unpublished, may throw an astonishing light on the emotional adventures of Stephen Crane, and especially upon his significant break from the ruling moral code.

Ford, 'By God! When Stevenson wrote "With interjected finger he delayed the action of the timepiece," meaning "He put the clock back," Stevenson put back the clock of English fiction one hundred and fifty years!'

The adventure of the Spanish-American War lured Crane for a year. It was as if he searched in vain for the moments of unearthly terror in the *Red Badge*, and found instead the confused bustle of quartermaster maneuvers, the emptiness of actual engagements. It was for the last time; exposure and fever had broken his health, and one finds it significant that he returned to England in 1899 with the intention of fixing himself there permanently. On the whole he was happier: he had found a more sophisticated public for his work; he had received great encouragement from English writers; his position was one of greater personal freedom and less absurdity than in America.

He now took, on the advice of a friend, Brede Place, 'an immense haunted and unrestored Elizabethan manor house, lying unhealthily beshadowed and low in a Sussex valley.' Here it was hoped that the perfect quiet and freedom, as his wife put it, 'from a lot of dear good people,' would be beneficial, since his great difficulty was 'a lack of that machine-like application which makes a man work steadily.'

He had artisans come and replace the old ironwork, while leaving the ancient sagging floors quite as they had been. There were candles everywhere preserving the dimness of 1398. He had found, he had been touched at last by *atmosphere*, something which was nowhere to be met with in the United States. Was it not for this atmosphere that thousands of Americans crossed the seas and scoured Europe? He led here the life of an Elizabethan baron. 'Rushes covered the floor,' Ford Madox Ford relates. 'Dogs lay beneath the table to gnaw the bones that fell; a baron of beef and a barrel of ale stood always near the back door for every tramp to consume. The house was filled with stray dogs, lost cats, and, as if in tides, indiscriminately chosen bands of irresponsible guests would fill and recede from the half-furnished rooms. . . .'

And in a small room above the great porch Crane would sit alone writing at twenty pounds per thousand, to keep it all going. Those who looked on and watched the deathly-pale young man filling in his steady, tiny writing the long sheets of foolscap in a gallant and vain attempt to sustain that immense, decaying house and its uncalculated hospitality, could have wept for pity. There was a horse, there were perhaps two horses, on which he went riding about the country. But always the tides of people whom Cora and Stephen Crane attracted turned up from London at all hours, slept on the floors or in corners, kept up the interminable rounds of drinking.

This was Stephen Crane's literary life in England. He teemed with ideas, he had vast designs for plays and novels. He needed solitude above all, but was betrayed by his liking for the scene of sheer human confusion in troops and crowds. And so he wrote what was first at hand, while his thirty dogs and puppies slept in his study, or demanded to be put outside—with the eternal glass of ale at his elbow, for the daily, or whenever, twenty pounds, since he was popular and lucky. And the great plans were steadily pushed back or laid aside for the future.

He was lucky? But how largely the tale of the American artists becomes one of 'broken careers, orphaned children, early disasters, violent deaths,' as Henry James had noted in another category. The bright air of the happy and pushing land would go on furnishing so much fantastic, fugitive, and heavy-hearted genius! How often the American abroad, intoxicated by the taste of European liberties, collapsed in fiber and frame. Stephen Crane's disposition had always urged him to shun neither temptation nor danger; and now his life approached its dreadful and premature term. Sick, and heavily in debt everywhere, he fell into a panic and worked with vain haste.

4

Henry James, living within calling distance at Rye, looked on his young compatriot with compassion. In 1897—he was now in fullest middle age—he had fallen in love with Sussex and gone to live for good in his charming old Lamb House at Rye, all furnished in Chippendale and Sheraton. It had a small garden and lawn, 'the whole hemmed in by a peaceful red wall, plentifully tapestried by espaliers.' The lovely tower of Rye Church looked down into it, as Edmund Gosse describes it, and James felt that the chimes sounded sweetly to him as he faced his garden in monastic quiet, the little market town with its cobbled streets packed tightly about him, yet out of sight.

He had changed much, and externally, during the long years of expatriation. For some reason, Mr. Ford Madox Ford tells us, 'just as Shelley used to call himself The Atheist, he loved to appear in the character of a sort of Mr. Pickwick—with the rather superficial benevolences, unctions, and the mannerisms of which he was perfectly aware. In his conversation there was a chuckling, savoring, enjoyment of words.'

And William James notes, toward 1890, 'He has covered himself like some marine crustacean with all sorts of material growths, rich sea-weeds, and rigid barnacles and things, and lives hidden in the midst of his strange, heavy alien manners and customs.' But these were all but 'protective resemblances,' under which the same dear old innocent and at bottom very powerless-feeling Harry remained, caring for little but his writing, and full of affection for all gentle things.

William had pleaded with his brother, by letter and during the amusing collisions of his visits to Europe, to return. 'Europe,' he would say, 'all the sweet decay . . . has produced a sort of physiological craving for a change to robuster air.'

It was in vain. Henry James, moreover, had a secret source of strength which preserved him in the rather anomalous, corruptive atmosphere of a cosmopolitan life. His strength lay in his consistency and his faithfulness. Virtually nothing had happened to him, by contrast with such a youth as Stephen Crane's, save the long arduous march toward the further secrets of his literary art. He had largely renounced society, while he practiced what the natives and servants of Rye deemed was black magic, since they could see him emerge from behind his walls for his daily promenades with rolling eyeballs and scowling brow. And surely there was magic in the stories of his late manner, as he composed now, in a certain luxury and release that he had never known: *What Maisie Knew*, *The Turn of the Screw*, *The Altars of the Dead*. There was magic above all in those stories of the literary life such as the *Lesson of the Master* and the *Figure in the Carpet*, in which the life of art was set proudly against the life of barter and trade, and was at the same time imbued with a pattern, a luminous, symbolic secret of its own, madly sought both by the characters of his fictions and by the readers thereof!

For this richer, inward life within an ivory tower James had made certain sacrifices of worldly advantage. Toward 1890 he had felt himself fallen on evil days, as he wrote to Howells. He had felt utterly lonely on the 'literary plane'; and when he viewed the sixpenny humbug that was being produced in America and consumed in such numbers he turned upon himself in despair. His brilliantly wrought novels had won the slenderest of publics, and now he not only felt this waning, but perceived with bitterness that his position in society had been weakened by the long period of insuccess, that he was being steadily forgotten. In a last effort for worldly success, the desire for which he did not conceal, he had planned to invade the theater. With the utmost deliberation and pains, a half dozen plays were composed, over a series of years, with which he hoped to eclipse the fame of his hated colleague, Oscar Wilde, the strange celebrity of the hour. The climax had come on the night of January 5, 1895, with the production of *Guy Domville*, a delicate and picturesque play which had the disadvantage of leaving all the threads of the plot as loose as they would be in life. A constellation of artistic, literary, and scientific celebrity had gathered at the St. James Theatre, and George Alexander, the famous player and director, was confident of success. All of James's hopes and fears were keyed up to an excruciating pitch. But when the curtain fell for the close and he was called to appear, a storm of hoots, catcalls, and jeers had greeted him from the gallery, 'the whole producing the effect of hell broke loose.' And the author, 'white as chalk,' as Edmund Gosse relates, 'bowed and spread forth deprecating hands' and then vanished in silence, mopping his brow. It did not matter that it was an effort to humiliate Alexander through a cabal, rather than James; he was through. And he was reported to have slept splendidly once the thing was over. He had withdrawn to the country with a wholly resolute attitude toward his public and his own 'mission.'

Like Henry Adams (who lived out his old age as a recluse in Paris), James now fortified himself by contempt for the principles and taste of the world outside. The only hope, as these two older Americans expressed it in a curious correspondence, resided in accepting the limited number of survivors, the 'one in a thousand,' as their medium. But if the great public ignored the master, if popular magazines no longer dared to print his novels, he found by compensation a purer fame. In the late '90s, a contemporary relates, all the literary pilgrimages were made either to George Meredith or Henry James. James seemed to live upon a plateau which he ruled over magisterially.

In this later period, James had undergone a further evolution which drew him far from the French realists of his youth. Ignoring Mayfair and its dinner and tea-parties to which he had come with faithful notebook for so many years, he labored now over his great triad of novels: *The Ambassadors, The Golden Bowl, The Wings of the Dove.* He was no longer an apologist for realism; for clearly, his tendency now was to idealize life in a classical sense. Life itself, photographed, recorded in raw or palpitating 'slices,' no longer concerned him. It was only what you did with the slices that mattered; the great artist must do something with life. The naturalists, he held now, had nothing to show us in the way of operation of character, the possibilities of conduct, the part played in the world by the *idea.* Therefore he preferred Hamlet and Lear as characters, because they were so 'finely aware' of what was happening to them, whereas most ordinary people weren't aware of anything. In the last novels he clings skillfully to the plausible, but idealizes his characters by endowing them with an extraordinary sensitiveness, consciousness, with a wealth of human grace and complexity, obviously drawn from his own strange organism.

These glowing volumes of his maturity, on which he lavished so many golden words, exquisite scenes and conceits, were primarily written for *initiates,* and led to his being termed 'the novelist's novelist.' He had made a splendid effort to lift subject above the level of mere anecdote, to place it within the sphere of drama through a design that was at once simple and dignified, while thanks to his elaborate, polyphonous style, objects and people appeared both with density and softness of outline, and actions had an extraordinary time-value. For those who were willing to grant patience, obedience, to hand themselves over to the master, these novels offered the highest drama. Having granted a reciprocating intensity of attention, one could accept then the seriousness, the delicacy and integrity of character; one became hypnotized by the slow passion, the majestic and muted music of the prose.

'It is art that *makes* life,' he wrote at the end, 'makes interest, makes importance . . . and I know of no substitute whatever for the force and beauty of its process!'

The 'later manner' was much deprecated, and not least by William James. His frank democratic heart must have been vexed and affronted by such an art, and he has well expressed the standard disapproval of his brother's last works.

'You know how opposed,' he wrote, 'your whole "third manner" of execution is to the literary ideals which animate my crude and Orson-like breast, mine being to say a thing in one sentence as straight and explicit as it can be made, and then to drop it forever; yours being to avoid putting it straight, but by dint of breathing and sighing all round and round it, to arouse in the reader who may have had a similar perception already (Heaven help him if he hasn't!) the illusion of a solid object made (like the "ghost" at the Polytechnic) wholly out of impalpable materials, air, and the prismatic interferences of light, ingeniously focused by mirrors upon empty spaces. . . . But . . . the method seems perverse,' he concludes. '*Say it out, for God's sake, and have done with it!* And so I say, give us *one* thing in your older direct manner, just to show that you can still write according to accepted canons. Give us that interlude; and then continue like the "curiosity of literature" that you have become. For gleams and innuendoes and felicitous verbal insinuations you are unapproachable, but the *core* of literature is solid. Give it to us *once* again! The bare perfume of things will not support existence [wrote the pragmatist], and the effect of solidity you reach is but perfume and simulacrum.'

To which Henry James replied stoutly that he would 'consider his bald head dishonored' if ever William came to be pleased by anything he wrote, and that the elements of his subject matter had no 'analogy with the life of Cambridge,' that he could not write by the 'two-and-two-make-four' system, and that it all showed 'how far apart and to what different ends (very naturally and properly!) we have had to work out our respective intellectual lives.'

5

And now benevolently he called upon his gifted young compatriot of Brede Place, finding him in the tumult of his perilous 'success' the dupe of countless impossible persons who fed on him and spoke ill of him in London. James had once, in London, had a bad hour in a visit with Crane, during which his host had carefully removed him from a party in full progress to an adjoining room, where they had talked about literature. But in the meantime, a notorious Madame 'Zipango,' present in the party, had ruined James's silk hat beyond repair by filling it with champagne; it was all Crane could do to rescue the hat and get the lady out of the hotel. Mr. James had made a 'holy show of himself in a situation that would have been simple to an ordinary man,' and yet Crane found it impossible to dislike him. He was so kind to everybody. . . .

And Crane, for his part—except for lapses when he would speak of James as 'Henrietta Maria' and damn his late friend, Stevenson, and the whole parlor game of literature in England—could be boyishly respectful and enthusiastic about the Old Man. He could be enchanted by a sentence of the master's uttered at a flower show, that had thirty clauses and some nine parentheses. He admitted even to having learned much from James's criticism of the French novelists.

To Henry James, however, Stephen Crane appeared to have 'lived with violence.' He had 'the manners of a Mile End Roader,' and yet was 'of the most charming sensitiveness . . . so truly gifted . . . so very lovable.'

A whole long generation, more than thirty years, had passed since James had come to stay permanently in Europe. He had seen all the great nineteenth century Americans with whom he had been linked pass away. Emerson was dead; and Lowell was gone, and Charles Norton. And here was an extraordinary young man who came in a later pilgrimage than his to bridge the void, and was thus an object of the utmost curiosity. The later United States, the incredible, sprawled, and blatant democracy, was in his manner, in his New Jersey accent, in his somewhat disheveled career, in his thirst for sensations to compose a life of 'action.' In a wholly American way his talent had sprouted swiftly, almost unconsciously, escaping moral traditions and discipline such as Henry James had invoked, and yet seizing with intuition the spirit and the methods that were in the air of the day. Would Crane go on forcing the world to read his formless but keenly perceived 'slices' of real life? Would he go on flourishing in English soil while his outlandish manners were forgiven, while doors opened and difficulties solved themselves as if without effort on his part? Or was there some fatality in the case of the American exile, as James had presented it long ago in *Roderick Hudson,* which doomed him to an early blight? One could look at Stephen Crane, as Joseph Conrad said, and perceive that he had not the face or the manner of a lucky man.

But when some one called Crane 'Baron Brede,' then Henry James turned furious.

'Figure to yourself,' he would say to Ford Madox Ford, 'what would be *your* feelings, if being, as I hope I may phrase it, an honored guest in Baltimore or one of our friend Wister's gentler southern cities, you should find installed in a place of honor, but laughed at as a peculiar national representative of your own, some—gifted, I grant you: oh, surely gifted—but wholly atrocious for accent and mannerisms—Cockney from the Mile End Road!'

What appalled him was the mockery which poor Crane made of the life of a Tudor lord—on the poor twenty pounds per thousand words! The Old Man shuddered to see a settled and august mode of European existence reduced to absurdity; and it was all the more painful because that 'very mockery was the sincere expression of admiration by a compatriot.'

But the old beams of Brede Place were now falling in ruins upon the head of its unfortunate host. The 'bohemian stronghold' held a thunderous New Year's party to usher in the twentieth century, and it was reported in London as a 'Babylonian orgy.' Stephen Crane appeared hurt and depressed. His very guests spread his ill-repute in London, having used his hospitality. The same scandal-mongering that had made New York intolerable pursued him in London. Was there no escape then from the consistency of human nature? He had hoped, ingenuously, to find in Sussex his own 'Great Good Place,' where he might live with amenity, gayety, and joy in his labor. . . .

There were rumors of Crane's leaving England. Would he return to the States? But one day, in the early spring, he spat blood and fell ill of his last protracted disease.

He was beyond the aid of solicitous friends. Henry James extended himself for 'poor dear Stevie,' showing depths of mystic benevolence. His concern, according to Ford, was fantastic; 'he turned his days into long debates—and he lay all night awake fearing that he might have contemplated something that might wound or patronize the boy. He would run the gamut of grapes, public subscriptions, cheques. He cabled to New York for sweet corn and soft-shell crabs to get the boy home food. And when they came he threw them away—for fear they should make him more homesick!' He said of Stephen Crane, 'I loved him so. . . .'

They saw Crane at Dover as he lay by a hotel window looking out at the pale green sea of the Channel. It wasn't bad, he said. He was sleepy, and only a little curious as to which world he was in. They rushed him to the Black Forest in Germany, in a vain race against death, and he lingered for some weeks there until June had come.

VIII

THE RETURN OF HENRY JAMES

THERE was an interval when Henry James, as an old man, could look back with renewed hope to his native land which he had forsaken thirty years ago in order to vibrate more finely in the presence of the European oracle. In his yearning youth he had departed in quest of impressions more various and more intense than those he might gather on the native scene. But after long years in the very precincts of the temple the divine voice had seemed to lose its note of mystery and augustness; and it curiously befell 'that the native, the forsaken scene now passing, as continual rumor had it, through a thousand stages and changes, and offering a perfect iridescence of fresh aspects, seemed more and more to appeal to the faculty of wonder.'

It was American civilization, in the twentieth century, that had begun 'to spread itself thick and pile itself high.' He heard of Brobdingnagian feats in iron and stone; he heard of Babylonian towers and industrious monsters of steam and fire; and vast deserts changed into peopled groves, and bristling cities arisen on the prairies, and such tales of the wealth of Midas and the power of Rome that he speculated deeply upon what rich opportunities might have been lost in the course of a long voluntary absence.

Having augmented the long tale of his fiction by a series of great novels, *The Ambassadors, The Wings of the Dove, The Golden Bowl,* James, at sixty, felt the need of pause and a turn to fresh fields. He had clung to that which he knew, that with which he was saturated; the last novels had drawn again and again upon the international scene, and upon those Americans and Europeans of the finer grain who played out their beautiful game in the complex pages. The last novels were, in effect, exquisite pleadings for humanism, for sensitiveness almost as an end in life. Their reality and their force depended largely upon the susceptibility of the reader to the Jacobin narcotic: once you embarked upon these novels, as a brilliant disciple said, they provided you with a fine-spun web of emotions in which you might run hither and thither like a distraught spider. But you could as well conceive these novels as taking place in the Venusberg as in London or Venice, so little did the feeling of soil enter into them. And, plainly, he felt the need for 'contact with his soil'—although the human heart had proven to be the same universally, and one would have enjoyed as well James's meditations on the soul of a Polynesian or an Afghan, for their intrinsic richness and brilliance. There was also the sense of fatigue and ennui after the exertions of his ripest years; and in the silence of his 'ivory tower' Henry James now bewailed the absence of all adventure upon the surface of life, beyond his few voyages. He has Strether, in *The Ambassadors,* speak revealingly for him: 'There were "movements" he was too late for—weren't there, with the fun of them already spent? There were sequences he had missed, and great gaps in the procession: he might have been watching it all recede in a golden cloud of dust. . . .'

To friends he recalled touchingly the graces of an early New England society; he declared himself homesick for New England smells and even sounds, and regretted as well the 'excellent conversation' that could have been heard in Washington thirty or forty years ago. In seeing some friends off at Tillbury Dock recently, he had reached a state of rare excitement. 'Once aboard the lugger . . .' he murmured; 'and if . . . say a toothbrush and something for the night— By Jove, I might have—'

In these years he sometimes felt poignantly the deficits of the cosmopolitan life and we find him urging his brother William to contract for his sons 'local saturations and attachments in respect to their *own* great and glorious country, to learn, and strike roots into, its infinite beauty, as I suppose, and variety. Then they won't, as I do now, have to assimilate, but half-heartedly, the alien splendors—inferior ones too, as I believe—of the indigestible Midi of Bourget and the Vicomte Melchior de Vogüé, kindest of hosts. . . . But make the boys stick fast and sink up to their necks in everything their *own* countries and climates can give *de pareil et de supérieur*. Its being their "own" will double their *use* of it. . . .'

Edith Wharton, whose *Valley of Decision* was dedicated to him, he warned 'not to go in too much for the French or the Franco-American subject.' He would like to tether her in native pastures, 'even if it reduced her to a backyard in New York!'

He planned for the future an American novel, as he told Howells, reinforced by observation, imagination, and reflection, now at their maturity. He was hungry for 'material' and felt persuaded of possessing great advantages for the adventure: he would be 'fresh' as any stranger by virtue of his long absence, while remaining as acute as an initiated native.

And now he breathed and hovered over the idea of a return, quite like one of the tremulous personages of his fictions. He 'gloated' in advance over all the awaited sensations, and actually announced to William James his intentions some two years prior to the act. If he went at all he must go before it was too late, before he was too old. It was the only chance that remained to him in life of anything that might be called a *movement:* 'my one little ewe-lamb of exotic experience, such experience as may convert itself . . . into vivid and solid *material*, into a general renovation of one's too monotonized grab-bag.'

William cautioned him. He knew his brother well, and offered reservations of the utmost delicacy: 'I feel keenly a good many of the *désagréments* to which you will be inevitably subjected; and I imagine the sort of physical loathing with which many of the features of our national life will inspire you.' If Henry were coming to the United States, he warned him darkly, he must be prepared to see his fellow beings in hotels and dining-cars eat boiled eggs broken in two by a negro and served with butter! And then concluding with a metaphysician's touch, 'I should hate to have you come and feel that you had now done with America forever, even in an ideal and imaginative sense, which after a fashion, you can still indulge in.'

But Henry James persisted stoutly. 'What you say of the Eggs (!!!),' he replied, 'of the Vocalization, of the Shocks in general, is utterly beside the mark—it being absolutely *for* all that class of phenomena . . . that I nurse my infatuation. I want to see them. I want to see everything.' He wanted in fact to see the whole strange country—in *cadres*, in sections, as complete and realized as those of the celebrated Taine, when he went to Italy in order to write his *Voyages*. He wanted to see the west and the south and even, dreamably, Mexico! And all this travel was to be an adventure, swiftly carried off, imbued with the poetry of motion. For the 'actual, bristling

U.S.A.' now had the merit and the property of fitting in with his creative preoccupations.

His memory grew vivid of Fresh Pond in Cambridge, where he and Howells had discoursed in a row-boat; it played upon sophisticated Newport with its refined inhabitants of fifty years ago, who had just returned from the grand tour; and it hung farther back over the autumn of New York and the October leaves that one's feet stirred in the quiet walks of Washington Square.

2

His mind was open, his senses on the alert. There were none, for that matter, more sensitive than he to the new social values, the new legends. His long sojourns in the older lands had made for intense reflection on human history and human possibility, so that he might measure all the better the civilization which had grown so heedlessly here. He braced himself against the expected avalanche of impressions that would bring tumbling both memories and anticipations.

'I would take my stand on my gathered impressions,' he said, 'since it was for them, for them only that I returned: I would, in fact, go to the stake for them—'

Strange pilgrimage! This man who was all insight and conscience, all concerned with ends and consummations, stirred alone from his foreign anchorage to record, to spy upon, the vehement young anarchy which gave so little thought, in the tumult of the present, either to its conscience or to its tomorrows. The adventure was to result in his writing *The American Scene*, the travel diary of a 'restored absentee' who wanders through his unrecognizable land and gives words to his deception and his terror. The unflattering, difficult work, which has been forgotten by a generation, brims with his accumulated impressions; its admonitions, its prophecies, are sound. Henry James, for all his fear of dogma, for all his manner of endlessly qualifying, had a fixed concept of civilization; he had the convictions which had upheld men of his type more or less since the fifteenth century in Italy. And when we remember that his far-off youth in New York and New England was rooted in a more innocent epoch, before the industrial revolution, we may understand the deep misgivings in these pages, the overtones of fear and impotence. He gives way to no loud, unrestrained lamentations or spectacular wringing of hands. It was simply a world by which he felt himself and his fellows forever excluded and condemned. One might protest if only revolt had seemed valid—but he perceived too well, too definitely, the resistless triumph of the 'barbarous' order.

The *drama*, as he saw at the first glimpse, would be 'the great adventure of a society reaching out into the apparent void for the consummations, after having earnestly gathered in so many of the preparations and necessities.' He fled directly from the littered waterside of New York Bay to the depths of New England where he could enjoy for the summer the true rusticity of New Hampshire forests, lakes, and hills, an ample and lovely countryside, to which, the artist in him protested nevertheless, 'nothing had been done' by men. But New York, the 'appalling and elaborately dire' metropolis of his birth, haunted him. He returned and thought that he could view along the Hudson 'the scattered members of a monstrous organism, flinging abroad its loose limbs even as some unmannered young giant at his "larks."' Formidable New York, behind which the colossal nation gathered itself, cried out its appeal and its character unmistakably in that note of vehemence which bespoke 'a particular type of dauntless power.' The *will to grow* was everywhere written large, and to grow at no matter what or whose expense. This was the overpowering idea with which the 'monstrous form of Democracy' now rumbled on; and it was borne to him by the motion and expression of every floating, hurrying, panting thing, by the throb of ferries and tugs, the glint of lights, and the shrill of whistles. And he saw plainly how the whole organism was caught in all its members by a bold lacing together of wire and steel web, which took on the complexity of some 'colossal set of clockworks, some steel-souled machine-room of brandished arms and hammering fists and opening and closing jaws.'

James's criticism, as one resumes it from the ill-organized ruminations and metaphors of *The American Scene*, plays upon two signal aspects: the gregarious, moral customs which the mechanized society tended to, and the unconscionable tempo at which life was lived. Both conditions succeeded in stamping out all that individual liberty which democratic theory had originally had in view.

The eternal lift on which you are rushed to the upper regions became a symbol of the 'herded and driven state.' To move perpetually in a human bunch, hustled in military drill, at the imperative order to 'step lively,' into the tight mechanical box that slides and slams in your rear as ruthlessly as the guillotine—what a price this puts on seclusion and privacy, on the sense of independent motive power! In the end free existence and good manners seemed to exist only in marginal relation to the 'endless electric coil, the monstrous chain that winds around the general neck and body, the middle and legs, very much as the boa-constrictor winds around the group of the Laocoön.'

He communes now with the multitudinous skyscrapers 'standing up to view . . . like extravagant pins in a cushion, already overplanted, and stuck in as in the dark, anywhere and anyhow.' Impudently new and impudently 'novel,' they had the air of being surprised at themselves. He felt profoundly the note of the merely *provisional* twinkling at him from the 'thousand glassy eyes of these Monsters of the Market.' Crowned by no history and consecrated by no uses save the commercial, he wondered ingenuously if they were not waiting to be 'picked' off by time, when science had some greater card up its sleeve. The word would perhaps be, then, for building from the earth's surface downward? Certainly the skyscrapers of 1904 reflected no interested passion seeking beauty, or the final form of beauty, as one felt this in Giotto's bell-tower of Florence. Nor did the 'giants of the mere market' recall as yet the builded majesties of the world as hitherto known in temples, fortresses, and palaces. Whatever primitive and potential beauty they held was veiled for the repatriated wanderer who saw with dismay only the force of obliteration in them. The famous old spire of Trinity seemed submerged in a deep, dark well, as he staggered, in Wall Street, by the wide edge of the whirlpool. (He did not lose sight of the fact that the very trustees of the great church had consented to its humiliation by disposal of the adjacent land owned.) Here then, at the frenzied corner where Broadway receives from Wall Street the 'fiercest application of the maddening lash,' he felt not only poor Trinity Church cutting a wretched figure, but himself, the brooding, pedestrian analyst, the strayed reveler, bending under the bitterness of history. The new landmarks, in the name of economic expansion, stamped out the old. But what was most terrible was that the old landmarks which were momentarily spared, and with which one's ties had been formed, contained in a tragic contrast a 'whole condensed past.' And the impact of this produced a horrible sense of personal antiquity.

Did not a great cold shadow throw itself over the architecture of his own prose, over the already outmoded beauty of his many volumes? What form of art could encompass, could realize the sense of, this new scheme of life? The buildings were in themselves huge, constructed and compressed communities, throbbing through myriads of arteries and pores with their passion. And now he thought of great wonder-working Emile Zola, with '*his* love of the human aggregation, of the artificial microcosm, which had to spend itself on shops, businesses, apartment-houses of the inferior, of the mere Parisian scale. . . .' What if *Le Ventre de Paris* or *Au Bonheur des Dames* could have come into being under the New York inspiration? Such love for humanity in the teeming mass, he, for his part, as he implies by accent, did not share. He stood condemned to become invisible under the vast money-making structure. For his own purpose was comparable only to that which conceived the Trinity spire—sinking under the pitiless law of growing invisibility for cathedrals.

He stared at the thousand windows, at the apertures into which mobs fought their way, as at a world of immovably closed doors behind which immense 'material' lurked, material for the artist, the painter of life, who had begun 'so early and fatally to fall away from possible initiations.' He stared with the sense of a baffled curiosity, *an adventure forever renounced.* Assuredly a vast amount of movement and of life clamored for admission into his mind, as he had seen the mob fight for life at the entrance of an electric car. But there was a limit to what the imagination could contain and absorb. He could no longer understand what every one, what any one, was really doing. Save that—at the mouth of Wall Street you saw the breath of existence simply taken on the run.

All the monstrous phenomena, he concludes, struck him *as having got the start, got ahead of any possibility of poetic, of dramatic, capture.*

Impossible to neglect the meaning of this phase of James's personal drama. At this moment it is extremely tempting to see in Henry James the hoary and symbolic figure of the Rip Van Winkle legend which America eternally offers. He has survived a whole foundered generation and returned alone as the appealing, the dominant, figure of an unfortunate, tragic class which had neither understood nor been understood by its people. Its members had been driven into exile or into the silence of confinement.

There had been a profound division of spirit, a muffled but no less passionate rebellion which James, mild, suave, resigned as he was, clearly typified. The final sense of the situation as it came to him was that which had come to all of the others in turn; the phenomena of the new civilization, for them, were beyond capture in artistic form.

3

Whoever departs from his native city or hamlet for a long voyage (or falls under a lasting enchantment) must pay the penalty upon returning of witnessing the heavy and melancholy changes of time. But the New City of unceasing change passed all bounds. It projected itself to our aesthetic Rip Van Winkle as practically 'a huge, fifty-story conspiracy against the very idea of the ancient graces.'

There, from Bowling Green, he glimpsed suddenly the old Castle Garden where, as a boy, he had been taken to hear the infant prodigy, Adelina Patti, and a whole firmament of long-extinguished stars. The commodious concert hall, which for long decades had been a conspicuous 'value' in the life of the city, was now diverted to other strange uses, shabby, shrunken, barely discernible for the league-long bridges and the skyscrapers.

He stopped before a low, faded brick house on the south side of Waverly Place which had been the small school attended by him in the almost mediaeval costume of his boyhood. On the other side of the square a high, impersonal office-building had utterly suppressed the house of his birth in Washington Place.

It was not as if he did not derive some humor from the grotesque situation. Inwardly he had always placed a little tablet which commemorated his birth at this spot. But of what use, of what visibility, he asks in mock despair, is a memorial tablet set against a fifty-story façade? A new life shaped itself now as one largely preoccupied with 'things'; but they were things to which no human attachment could be formed, as in other times. How could one become fond of an old elevator, for instance, as one might of an old staircase which beloved feet had trodden? You discarded the outworn machine without sentiment. . . .

The whole of lower Fifth Avenue, from the little Washington Arch to Fourteenth, every block of which was preciously remembered, lay as under a doom. Here was a sadly altered Union Square, once fenced in by an iron grill, and now no longer safe for children to play in. And here on Fourteenth Street the parental home and the familiar brownstone church of other years were vanished from sight forever!

He paused before this particularly painful place in his memory and looked backward at the whole 'renounced adventure.' What would he have been? he asked himself. What would he have been if he had stayed?

He remembered the large high rooms, the stairway of checkered marble. He remembered the parlor with its many pictures, the friendly fireside before which Emerson had sat, and Ripley and Curtis and Dana, and earlier still Washington Irving and even the ill-starred Poe. He remembered the bright rooms above, which had brimmed with the sound of the children's study and play. And then instead of growing up slowly to become a part of the big, native aggregate, to be stamped and cast in the standard mold, he had gone far away, as far as possible, to worship at foreign shrines.

Such speculations over ghosts and destinies and the vanished crossroads of a life are contained in the story called *The Jolly Corner*. Here the writer reveals himself to us in a mood of confession, stirred by the remembered places revisited, the fated youth relived.

Spencer Brydon, absentee from his native New York for thirty-three years, returns to look after his property on which he has lived abroad. He finds everything a 'surprise'; values and proportions are all upside-down. The property is the great house on the jolly corner of the Avenue—the one in which he had first seen the light, in which the various members of his family had lived and died. He is now engaged in various projects of dismantling and rebuilding, in order to 'keep pace with progress,' and he finds himself absorbed in these problems. The faculty for construction, for enterprise, so typical of the native environment, may have been, in truth, dormant in him; but in all his life abroad it had been withheld, thrust back completely. His life, in fact, had been thoroughly guarded and insured against such gross preoccupations. And now he begins to wonder, as he roams through the huge, silent rooms which recall a faraway, an antediluvian and 'innocent' social period, what he might have become had he stayed.

'What would it have made of me? What would it have made of me? . . . I might have been . . . something nearer to one of those types who have been hammered so hard and made so keen by their condition. . . . I had then a strange *alter ego*, deep down somewhere within me, as the full-blown flower is in the small tight bud, and . . . I just transferred him to the climate that blighted him once and forever.'

He had, instead of staying to become one of those 'types'—one of the 'unmitigated business-faces' you saw in the street—followed strange paths, worshiped strange gods, and led these thirty years a 'selfish, frivolous, scandalous life.'

The story then takes place, one presumes, in the supernatural or really the fear-world of the dream. Spencer Brydon, harassed by the idea of his *alter ego*, still prowling somewhere in the environs of the old house, visits the place by night, lured by the 'presence' somewhere in the darkened rooms of his 'other self.' Helplessly drawn by his terror, which has endured through the whole night, he moves with a taper to the last inner room, whose door is meaningfully closed, and opening it finds him—seated, in full evening dress, hiding his face in his hands. The 'presence' lifts his hands, and in the moment before he faints, Spencer Brydon sees him—'spectral, yet human,' with a face of horror, ravaged, odious, blatant! . . .

4

William James, the beloved philosopher of Boston, had welcomed his brother with joy, foreseeing as a result of this journey a new lease of artistic life, 'with the lamp of genius fed by the oil of twentieth century American life.' Henry's visible reactions, however, which must have seemed so perverse to him, became a matter of keen disappointment. He did not fail to take him to task for the lacunae, the silences, the prejudices, with which his tale of the native culture was replete.

'I am surprised at you, Harry,' he would say. How could one fail to applaud the 'courage, the heaven-scaling audacity, and the *lightness*, withal, as if there was nothing that was not easy? And the great pulses and bounds of progress? . . .'

In the eternal strife between the two brothers, conducted on the plane of ideas, to be sure, and in face of the warmest mutual affection, there are clear suggestions of the whole intellectual dilemma of the period.

How deeply rooted William had become in his long and honorable New England career. He had effected a small revolution in science by his work in psychology. He had kept up a front that was moral, helpful, liberal and optimistic, no matter what came. Philosophy had flourished a little at Harvard under his leadership. But how anomalous the devotion to philosophy, the very persistence of philosophy, appeared in those times! Boston itself was anomalous; and its remoteness from the major currents of the national life was explained by the popular saying that 'Boston was not a part of America.' The very map showed you that all New England was a peninsula, and led you nowhere.

Most pathetic of all, however, were the moments when men like William James acknowledged their deception or despair; when they sensed the dissociation of intelligence and force, of the doctrines of reason or moral judgment and those of preëmption. The picture of William James and a few other professors holding a meeting of protest at the time of the Spanish-American War and debating what should be done lingers in the mind as minor American comedy, full of cruel overtones, which speak to us of the impotence of these intellectuals. The dissenters-for-an-hour would be forgotten, and they relapsed soon after to the unlovely level of a busy life filled with Chautauqua lectures and talks to ladies' clubs, while buoyed up by a sweet and uncritical faith in human nature, in free American institutions, and in the 'leaps and bounds of Progress.'

Clearly, those who were faithful and stayed to play their part lost something of their balance or perspective toward matters like Progress, while those who departed underwent heavy changes, and returning, seemed unhappy infidels so far as the gospels of Democracy were concerned.

Sheer change and expansion, mechanical and economic, subject to no plan in the name of human values, controlled by no authority—save that of predatory entrepreneurs—suggested itself to the detached gaze of exiles as a monstrous miscarriage of the affairs of men; a revolution of things that nullified completely the peaceful, disinterested labor of their class during four centuries.

Henry James wandered about the huge continent. He traversed unknown regions of the middle west and the far west; he penetrated deep into the south. It is legendary that he lectured from time to time in Philadelphia, Indianapolis, Kansas City, and elsewhere—the same lecture—before uncritical, provincial, and largely feminine audiences. Thus wherever he went he imparted his worldly wisdom, his humor, and his good taste, not to mention much specific comment that was pertinent and critical. One visualizes him tramping about Chicago on a bitter day, in his great British mackintosh, shuddering in the fierce gloom of the Loop. To the friend who accompanies him, he exclaims, 'Monstrous! Monstrous. . . .' Chicago, to him, was infinite, black, smoky, old-looking, like some preternaturally boomed Manchester or Glasgow, and putting forth railway antennae of maddening complexity and length.

The ugliness that flourished everywhere served as a fruitful theme; he traces it, in *The American Scene,* to the so complete abolition of *forms.* Could forms, tradition, authority, be introduced and developed, then ugliness might begin scarcely to know itself! The great cities of the new age were victims, in their swift growth without plan, without interspaces, of 'individualism,' as opposed to 'collectivism' and centralized authority. It would take so much effort in the future—and he was a good prophet—to recapture vistas, river banks, prospects of open water, from the grasp of the mills, the docks, and above all the railroads, which everywhere serenely asserted their priority over all other considerations.

In the face and aspect of the common people, he perceived with contentment the great lift from poverty in the United States. The living unit really had a sense of being a paying property in himself. But how signal was the loss of liberty, once this unit was confronted with other, much greater, properties, monopolies, combinations! And Henry James concludes with cruel candor: *There is freedom to grow up to be blighted.*

There were, to be sure, physical advantages aplenty in the new order of which James was quite sensible. Travel, movement, had its convenience and glamour. The 'Pullman' was only exceeded, in beauty and force, by the new 'chariot of fire,' as he called the automobile. He noted the rise of a new hotel civilization, grandiose, methodical, and gregarious, and predicted the disappearance of the outworn 'home' of his own boyhood in America! Yet everywhere one found his 'so excellent room with perfect bathroom and w.c. of its own, appurtenant. . . .'

It is significant that Henry James paused at Washington in his southward rush. The capital caused in him reflections of the greatest portent. Here, he thought, was a force which could, and once did, play the principal part in the direction of the people. Washington should have remained the theater of the Political Arts, inspiring, harmonizing, controlling. But he could no longer be hoodwinked. The capital was indeed a deliberately set stage, and of a splendid presence; yet nothing but shadow-play took place there. It existed by the tolerance of the markets and their monsters, and turning its back on these realities, hoped in vain that its conversations and discussions might be of some avail. . . . As a community of social leadership it yielded him only the sense of an aching void.

At length, after a year of peregrination, Henry James fled without regret. He was 'homesick' for his little anchorage in a corner of England. Certainly it was possible to live, to survive, in the United States; one could even earn more—but he was better, infinitely better, outside of it, far from the 'huge Rappaccini-garden,' as he humorously called it, 'rank with each variety of the poison-plant of the money-passion.'

In no sense did he nurse rancor against his native land, as so many have supposed. The tone of his letters in the last years indicates on the contrary a closer bond through new friendships, and a close connection with his family enhanced by the illness and death of William James and his own ill health. The changes which swept over the modern world, he must have perceived, would affect as heavily, in the end, the customs of Europe and of England. As a senile old man, although famous for his enduring charm, he passed his days in Lamb House, revising and prefacing the collected edition of his works. It was an enormous labor of love, lavished over many years upon an edition that was to be small and unprofitable. This work of technical exposition, written in his own elaborate-mannered style (which immediately frightened away the wrong people), shows how seriously James regarded his whole adventure as an artist, and how pathetically outmoded he seems in England too, during the new, undiscriminating times.

The prefaces were to be, as he wrote Howells, 'a sort of plea for Criticism, for Discrimination, for Appreciation on other than infantile lines. . . . They ought, collected together, to form a sort of comprehensive manual or *vade-mecum* for aspirants in our arduous profession.' With presages of mortality, he left to succeeding generations touching evidence of the great literary experimentation which had been conducted in Lamb House. There was the story of one's hero, he would say, and then there was also 'the story of one's story. . . .'

The conversion of Henry James into a British citizen in 1916, a few months before his death, has been a source of misunderstanding and injustice to the memory of the greatest American novelist. Henry James had always taken sides instantly, it must be remembered, in the 'war against culture' which he believed was being waged in his own country. But in 1914 it needed all his imagination to comprehend the scope of the disaster which had befallen the white races. He did comprehend. Like many of the poets, he was easily convinced that the prodigious military advance of the Germans was a 'war against culture' on a colossal scale. And so he was easily enrolled with men like Viscount Bryce, among the aged Defenders-of-the-Human-Spirit; and at seventy he found a new youth and ardor to write and speak of the war with a passion that astonished all those who knew him. He became transfigured during those dark years, reckoning everything lost for humanity and offering to throw his all into the crisis. It is in this way that old writers, who have lived very little, or only vicariously, are often overtaken by the 'historical impulse' in their declining days, and make *beaux gestes*. James's *beau geste* was to abandon voluntarily his American citizenship, in the effort to inspire other Americans like him to precipitate their country into the fight for culture on the western front.

Henry James had little interest in the cold bristling navy of England. He despised Kipling. It was simply that he imagined the triumph of the German arms would result in his old friend Edmund Gosse's being prohibited from writing essays, and his old friend John Morley's ceasing to write biographies, while one by one the precious books and objects in the British Museum would be given to the fire like the cathedral of Rheims.

IX

EXCURSION: THE AMERICAN SCENE

O Texaco Motor Oil, Eco, Shell, grandes inscriptions du potentiel humain! bientôt nous nous signerons devant vos fontaines, et les plus jeunes d'entre nous périront d'avoir considéré leurs nymphes dans le naphte.—L. ARAGON, *Le Paysan de Paris.*

WE MUST invoke the forbearance and the pardon of the reader for having painted in such decidedly melancholy tints the exotic, aborted, or estranged careers of American artists. Truly the men of the late nineteenth century were, for the most part, troubled souls; much evil befell them. And therefore we are in danger of pitying them.

Their ways were fugitive rather than rebellious. They were divorced from the spirit of their times; they were ill-suited for the dynamic States, and each in turn searched for a certain romance, for the richness of traditions, for a gentler civilization of which the signs, the 'paraphernalia,' were not visible in the immediate landscape. And since, in turn, the nation that hammered and shrilled with its jerry-building of an empire was equally unsuited for their rather delicate art, they fled in various directions. Their lives in the aggregate seem to compose a great pattern of flight.

Whistler, as we have seen, led a 'scandalous, frivolous life'; Henry Adams wandered about the world in search of his cherished Absolute; Bierce's was a career of violent gestures, vainly expended upon a mediocre stage; Lafcadio Hearn knew the cross of the uprooted soul, the eternal stranger, while the young Stephen Crane was early derelict by his own excesses. And Henry James, whose memories spanned the whole age, from the happy moment of the great New England group and the little New York of the Knickerbocker days to the abyss of the World War —Henry James, the lonely cosmopolitan of letters, had by his own confession missed his great chance to 'live,' and arriving at the station too late, could hear the train's far receding whistle miles and miles down the line. So many movements had passed him by, so many sequences, processions. . . . And yet we need be downcast no more by the tale of so much poignant effort than by the reddening and falling leaves of the deciduous trees. In fact we may grow positively exultant over those characters who listened to their hearts and, obeying their own nostalgias, set off on their long hunt for the Great Good Place. The destiny of the exile, we may be sure, was not an easy one; but we are overwhelmed by the accumulated evidence that the lot of the faithful, of those who clung to the earth of their country during this time, whether from preference or need, was infinitely harder.

In the end we must place the proper, delicate emphasis upon those issues of the affair that signify most for us. Which element was really shorn and betrayed of great intangible fortune, of potential gifts, endowments? Was it not really the people, the mass of Americans, who were most *deprived* in the last analysis? The immense rank and file, the vague throng of souls—is it not for them that we prefer to mourn, since life all about and within was automatically rendered less rich, less furnished and ornamented with so many possible meanings, values, stimuli, symbolisms, by the forced flight of the painters, men of letters, architects, philosophers, during a given era?

A perceptible *discontinuity*, a break, occurs in the whole descent of an American culture which had had interesting beginnings in the New England period. And so the resumption of the effort toward embellishing, toward consummating mere existence was to become all the more faltering and laborious in the century that followed. There would always be, thereafter, the spectacle of force dissociated from intelligence; ideas would take root but painfully, in the way of sensitive plants in a stony, impoverished soil; movements of thought would suffer periodic, successive breakdowns.

Indeed there has been much confusion in the whole matter of the American background. Even in the work of Mr. Van Wyck Brooks, which we must encounter seriously at almost every point, thanks to its excellent, intelligent, pioneering qualities, we find totally wrong implications. In his *Pilgrimage of Henry James,* Mr. Brooks concludes with a very hostile judgment of all the great novelist's later work, the work in which all his voyages and flights, and in fact his whole life, culminates. The great lesson, Mr. Brooks sternly concludes, is that one should not quit the native soil. We would not mitigate the difficulties of a disoriented, transplanted life. But strong suspicions arise, in the case of this critic, of a great deficit in taste when he sacrifices at least a dozen great volumes of prose to the needs of his thesis, volumes which by revenge now gain steadily in artistic life and influence for an English, French, and American posterity. Obviously the temperament of Mr. Brooks responds best to a highly moral literature, one that acts directly upon public opinion *by advocation* rather than indirectly by example. And if we assume, on the contrary, that the later work of Henry James must be placed among the finest literature of his time and signalizes him as the greatest American novelist, then his expatriation seems a very successful adventure, despite whatever sum of personal suffering imposed. What Henry James might have lost by living only vicariously was richly redeemed through his life in art. He who would write English prose today without reading the two great volumes of letters, mirroring all the interior movements of such a life—in the deepest sense, heroic—is simply to be pitied.

Edgar Poe's writings must first help form a Baudelaire, a Mallarmé, a Rimbaud, before they could really stir his own people. And so Henry James must first instruct and inspire a whole school of artists, Joyce, Virginia Woolf, T. S. Eliot, Marcel Proust, and many others, before he signifies much in his native New York. The test of a great American artist, as revealed by the case of Poe, Henry James, and even Whitman and Melville in lesser degrees, is whether he is *a good boomerang.*

It has often seemed to us that culture (like the disease, the teeming of microbes, which the word suggests) spreads best by contagion. There is no more cheering sign to our way of thinking than the phenomena of little poetasters, critics, dilettantes, snobs, ubiquitous in the local scene or period. It is at such moments that the informal, living, invisibly spreading university of art buzzes with young potentiality, rivalry, and even patronage. But there must be those who can teach, even if they breed only rebellion; there must be one or two masters. . . .

If we take the single aspect of culture represented by the birth and growth of a literary school, nothing strikes us as more fatal than the removal of the possible leaders in the whole game, the give-and-take, the intellectual competition, of the craft of writing. Now Henry James was peculiarly fitted, once you accepted personal idiosyncrasies, and nearly all of them on the side of human amiability, to be a 'master,' a dean of letters for younger artists. His self-discipline was most impressive; his fertility, his technical inventiveness, offered the most stimulating example; in fact his profound knowledge of the craft of fiction is only now beginning to be felt in proper measure. And so, one is persuaded that the discouragement, the expulsion not only of James but of his type, may have been one of the great, silent, unremarked calamities of the recent epoch.

The phenomenon of exile persists, today, as one of the secret maladies of American society. Is the emigration of intelligence to become an issue as absorbing as the immigration of strong muscle? With greater frequency than ever our *illuminati* buy tickets for a more possible world, for a more breathable air. In Mr. Ezra Pound, Miss Gertrude Stein, Mr. T. S. Eliot, and a numerous community of modern artists, we have established, chiefly in Western Europe, a brilliant legation of American talent. And whether it is to their liking or not, immediately behind them are the myriads of disciples, camp-followers, and sutlers who have all variously fled from their severe, ungrateful country. Everywhere in the Europe of today, along the streets of ancient cities, crooked or bowed down with history, along the favorable shores of that inland sea which cradled the great races, everywhere in solitary or nervous groups, spinning like fretful midges between two worlds, we have met those forlorn wanderers, those fugitives, those exiles.

We have seen exiles who, praying before some Bar, or shedding maudlin tears thereover, vowed with great oaths that they would never, never return to their fair land. We have seen other exiles arriving with paper and typewriter to make their dreary novels that will (outdoing Mr. Mencken!) expose the United States as an intolerable *Schlaraffenland* of boobery and buncombe. We have seen them embrace what you, Mr. Pound, term the 'old world view,' namely: 'that one is foolish to disturb one's leisure by taking thought or action, even to inquire into the possibility of saving a few fragments from the disjecta, or of starting a new plantation. . . .' We have seen them absorb an ingratiating and inexpensive Epicureanism. We have seen them admire and ape the manners of young Parisians, who take their rule from New York!—What a sign of the times this is, what an omen of decay! And we have seen them, in emulation of the more corrupt section of European society which accepts them, arise to the drums of jazz and dance, dance, to the overpowering rhythms of the American folk-music. . . .

The Europe to which they have fled is indeed a

hollow land: its oracles now speak mournfully of 'decline,' or of the 'Eastern torrents,' or of the 'failure of reason.' It is a continent harassed by its creditors, living virtually on half rations, where the new principles of power are thwarted by old national walls, where the halls of learning are still murmurous with those old enthusiasms and doctrines which led Europe to her bewilderment and disaster.

The penetration of jazz, the muse of primitive Americans, is of course but a parable of a larger economic invasion. It is not only the realm of pleasure and taste that is invaded (so that one sees Mr. Pound, the Composite Exile, mythically retreating ever farther, to the Balkans or the Carpathian ranges!) but we may perceive very well how the old social forms are being demolished by the new mass economics. On the surface we have decrepit republics, windy parliaments, or *la gloire* of comic opera, while the native music appears to be only the old songs of hate. . . . But for all this, the power of international cartels steadily introduces the American régime of quantity production, by which man becomes a paying economic unit rather than a political animal. We may see how the influence, the glitter, is submerged, of the Faubourg Saint-Germain, and all those genteel salons that once threw some silver pieces to the players and the philosophers. Landmarks tend, if not to disappear, then to become indistinct among the new mechanical images; the modern tempo certainly seizes upon the men of Europe; and moving now at the mean speed of sixty miles per hour, the glimpsed basilicas of the golden ages no longer bear the same proportions. Even from the Eternal City one comes away with a blurred vision of the altered Tiber valley: with the forms of St. Peter's and the Castel San Angelo there is queerly mingled that of a giant new metallic gas tank!

How perplexed the older American pilgrims would have been at the decline which appears to have overtaken the ancient graces of Europe. And no serious tourist who now retraces the journeys of his youth, or even of a few years previous, but gathers in an abiding sense of the threatened failure of old Europe as a last resort of leisure, individualism, personal freedom—as a place of escape.

We await, then, the slow forced return of the current. Many expatriates will retreat, disabused; and there will be increasing instances of Europeans completing their education in *Realpolitik* by visits to the American Imperium. We do not advance too promptly, too naïvely, for the immediate future, the hope of an American culture to be as predominant as American credit. For we have the habit of believing that Europe will recover her presently lost equilibrium; that even for the 'Machine Age,' with its conveniences and hazards, a finer human adjustment will be achieved in the end by the older societies, so that Europe will remain what she has always been:

a great reservoir of ideas. But then, the whole quality of the modern age is that of a greatly heightened international consciousness. The Atlantic, it has been noted, becomes, in our days, a Mediterranean Sea; and in the more rapid, uninterrupted exchange of ideas along its shores the American contribution is foreseen as at least more strategic, more vehement, than before.

We turn back after the lapse of a whole misled generation; we return, literally, to face again the American scene with our hopes and our demands. For the undeceived pilgrim there is the disappointment of being empty-handed, of having grasped vigorously almost at shadows in a void. But here the persistent, crushing sense comes over us that we are nearer to the seat of world-power; that for all the new ventures being staked, the new risks boldly incurred, we are so much closer to the destiny of peoples.

If we survive at all, we are prompted to ask ourselves: How much have we been coarsened and toughened that we survive? How many personal liberties, graces, by comparison with elder Americans and gentler Europeans, have we been forced to relinquish? . . .

The present transition—is America always, then, in transition?—seems the more violent, spectacular phase of the revolution of 1850-1865. There is the same optimism about progress, the same exclusive interest in the merely exploitable, the same economic confidence gripping the entire human mass at the crest of each 'bull market.' But one would guess, at the least, that the tempo of existence has been accelerated some three hundred per cent; and it is plain how the stamp of artifice, of mechanisms, on the whole complexion of life has grown deeper and harder. In this millennium of traffic, exquisitely controlled, of voluptuous bath-tubs, of ingenious airways, the development of social forms is felt to be toward an absolute and unified régime, toward collective rather than individual being.

Vain to weep or gibber, as Emerson doubtless would, at the corner of State and Madison, or Fifth and Forty-second; or as Whitman, who, in the 'talkies' of our time, would find the approved, the voiced, aesthetic-religious impulse of the mass. The colossal face of our great cities, so Egyptian in character, would offer to the libertarians and aesthetes of an earlier day only 'phenomena impossible of artistic capture,' phenomena impossible for *them,* at any rate, so that the passing of these men and their type seems fated.

The second half of the nineteenth century in America was hostile enough to the continuance of a cultural tradition, but the cultured, we must remember, were equally unfit for such a work, under the actual conditions. We are convinced nowadays that to have carried out the ideals of the worthy Transcendentalists would have needed the rigid closing of the country's gates, the destruction of the factories, the decimation of the citizens.

But the exiles of the Machine Age, at times, are also pathetic and ludicrous enough. Their dissociation from modern life has been no less thorough; their whole movement has been largely one of 'escape.' Mr. Pound, by turns, takes flight toward Provençal ballads, towards late Latin literature, toward Japanese art. Mr. Eliot escapes by way of old English divines and the *Summa Theologica* of St. Thomas. We are tempted to believe that both of these artists, who have vowed themselves to the cult of perfection, adopted such philosophies or religions as they have for the sake of purifying their art, or perhaps even of improving their style! And so it is amusing to think of the part they would now play in a society which has sometimes been called that of the New Barbarism. Such pure artists would appear to drop instantly to the rôle of pariahs. They would be cast into a lonely, feeble opposition to the whole order and all its social, mythological products. To be sure, an element of snobbery which now cheerfully raises its head in these States—and in itself a sign of civilization—might render them a flattering support. But no one knows what becomes of snobs in a time of war or social disaster. To please snobs alone does not impress us as the organic function of a great art. Under the American order which also seems to spread itself everywhere, the particular art of Mr. Eliot or of Mr. Pound seems threatened with extinction. One might go further and say that it bears the seeds of extinction within itself. For many of us have followed with faithful attention the progress of certain men toward the limits of their splendid, hermetical obscurity, of their unsocial, personal patterns of flight, and returned in the end with a bitter sense of the death of language. . . .

When we regard the kaleidoscopic film of present-day life the conviction grows that recent movements of art have recoiled from singularly great opportunities. The very nature of an era of quantity production and mass movements is tempting to all the qualities of leadership, enterprise, courage, which the Exiles have largely renounced. There is an abundance of new mediums, new organs whose appeal would surely not have gone unperceived by the inventive, experimental genius of the great ages. And under the multiform aspect of the New Barbarism, with its widely disseminated physical advantages and its spiritual griefs, remarkable sores and mysterious diseases take growth. The mass of men suffer profound new anxieties which are addressed by no adequate music and no philosophy.

It is the wonderful dissolution of values and authorities that gives the whole time its peculiarly liquid character. The power of the Church and of the University (as places of consolation or learning, surely) has dwindled: the system of Puritan restraints has passed as a moral code. Strangers quickly remark the notable failure of political authority, the flouting of laws, and, above all, the breakdown of the family institution. The new American woman is seen by them as a luxurious and stupefying creature whose 'rôle as mother, spouse, and guardian of the hearth scarcely exists. . . .' There are, moreover, strange manners or tribal customs protectively developed for this anonymous, gregarious world; there are unearthly trysting-places in the shaded catacombs of our subways; there are novel legends, bizarre heroes who appeal to us every day from the pages of illustrated journals, from cinemas and radio stations, so that we have a whole new mythology broadcast through all the machines of universal publicity.

In truth, individual disasters no longer concern us much; our news is of mobs slaughtered in tunnels or massacred in their sleep, carbonized in theaters or immolated on ferries. One hears even of a whole house, its supports sadly undermined, giving way and sliding, entire, into an adjacent excavation!

Sometimes the note of melodrama or hysteria sounds loudest above our impetuous activities and amusements. The flourishing of weird cults, the frequent waves of suicide, may be associated with a growing sense of deception which touches most contemporary thinking. On omnibuses one overhears adolescents discussing the 'failure of science.' And certainly it has 'got through' to great numbers of beings that the Victorian hopes have been dashed, of the complete, mechanically perfect knowledge of the natural universe which was to produce the successful therapy of all human ills as its final flower.

The present confusion of human values, the whole scene of foundered traditions and decaying institutions, may be largely blamed upon the immeasurable changes ordered by industrial revolution. (In the ulterior sense, a mechanistic philosophy of decades and centuries is actually at fault.) At any rate, changes, new rhythms, were introduced, for which no adequate moral resources were imaginable. We live now in a time of peace which has all the air of war.

Yet it is startling, once we leave the plane of ideas and sentiments, to perceive what rigorous discipline, what organization, implacable energy, novelty, prevails in the world of modern business and industry.

Here is an essential contradiction in the social scheme; and it speaks to us again of the tragic dissociation between force and intelligence. Human beings are seen only as paying industrial units. Aside from the exacted eight hours per day they have been left curiously to their own devices: unguided, uninspired as to their personal, inward life. For the whole emotional existence of the human creature, which begins and ends with the blast of a siren or the shutting and opening of a desk, only a negative authority has been allotted: the police. Is it merely the indifferentism of a pretendedly democratic policy that we feel, or is it at bottom a cynical, mechanistic view of human life? When we see our statesmen deliberating solely over matters of trade, tariff, or railroads, when we see them prohibit personal liberties only in the interests of 'efficiency,' then we infer, instead of mere apathy, a positive conception of man as an economic pawn. The result of such a policy for the extra-business life of the mass has been simply the impressive confounding of human values, all the interesting signs of corruption noted before. By its workings the energy of commerce is directed brilliantly from above; the moral tone is set from below.

Whatever sponsorship exists for the souls of men comes from a residue of industrial publicity, skillfully broadcast for the sweet sake of motor cars, tooth paste, silk stockings. . . .

This warping of natural emotions, resulting from a thoroughly mechanized order, can only bring some form of reaction or revulsion. Is it not time, then, to hope, to begin calculating the chances, for a kind of moral revolution? Men may grow tired of surviving as mere automatons. Only the simple, the ingenuous, the stupid, really believe that the present volume of noise all about us will be followed by a still greater quantity of detonations. As for the idea of speed, to be accelerated always, one ends by finding that absurd and indecent on the face of it, though it seem treason to say this. A period of reining-in must eventually come, to retard and check the whole pace of life, if there is to be any breath left with which to live. We shall cease then to let machines appear *to think for us* or determine what human needs shall be, whether populations shall thrive or famish.

Such a recoil, as one imagines it, would be attended by a Humanistic revival during which we would feel ourselves thrown back on our own resources. There would perhaps appear again, as in a cycle, a romantic search for the 'soul of man'; there would be an attempt to discover the traditional, historical qualities of *homo sapiens*, of man at his finest development, those qualities which have been admired in the past, those which we should like to see endure.

If, in approaching years, men may be more tempted to return to their natural emotions, one feels that they would not again be ruled by terror like the men of the Middle Ages. One would expect a growth of Humanism, with its system of discipline, proportions, intellectual perfection, rather than a return to fear-dominated religions. Despite the sense of being balked in so many directions, the real achievement of centuries of modern science has been the immensely superior physical dignity gained for the species. There has been too great a lift in the animal scale, too great a discovery of power and magic, for all men to become at once the children of fear.

One never stares at some hideous device of modernity without perceiving that the same energy could have made it lovely. One never recoils from the infinite ingenious products of hypocrisy, awkwardness, or cowardice, without the reflection that so much virtue, loyalty, superb vigor, elsewhere manifest, could have been brought to bear here, too. The possibilities of a change of morale are visioned, and are candidly urged if the very capacity for culture is not to be lost.

The Humanists believe in 'the freedom of the will to conform to a standard of values . . . that the rightful concern of man is his humanity, his world of value and quality that marks him off from a merely quantitative natural order.' But Mr. Henry Ford, who rules a social empire, plainly believes that men are nothing more than heaps of conditioned reflexes. Therefore the problem for Humanism, if it is not to remain always in the zone of academic debate, will be *the approach to power*.

The salvation and the strength of artists, in whom we have seen a potential force for Humanism, lies in their ability, hereafter, to incorporate themselves within the actual milieu. If a change of morale is imminent—as so many present signs may indicate to us, such as a growing respect for leisure in Florida, the appreciation of nudity and sunlight, the immense new appetite for music and dancing of a sort—then artists, too, may opportunely effect a *rapproche-*

ment. The idea may grow upon them that the machine itself is susceptible of a splendid usage: that only the soddenness of men destines it to effects of naïve horror. But in desiring a stronger sense of actuality, and a greater inventiveness (such as Bach exhibited in the perfecting of *The Well-tempered Clavichord*), in hoping that they may employ themselves, under a happier dispensation, with the rhythms of the cinema, the music of towers, the architecture of motor cars and shop windows, one does not necessarily expect campaigns to expel roaches or to mitigate or extend prostitution. The humanizing force of art may work best through example and symbol, upon the larger scale visioned, reaching numberless crowds through the magnificent new machines. Society may become collective, unified, directed by an absolute régime, as in Russia; but it may be nobly led.

A metamorphosis of such a nature, foreseen sometimes as more or less fatal, may appear grotesque, until we become accustomed to it. It need be drastic only upon the surface, however, while the eternal principles of art may be perceptible within: the form and technique of Gothic cathedrals, for instance, rather than their *manner*. So that the artists may become centurions of Soap for a time, pro-consuls of Hydro-electricity; they may improvise before the microphone, dance before the television box. A period of training, a phase of discipline, will elapse; and in the end the force of mind in them may again leaven this society which has known only material preoccupations. The dispersed and scattered beauty of automobiles and spotless kitchens and cubic office-buildings will have been organized and given meaning through their understanding of the ensemble. A spiritual equilibrium will have been reached in which they will have been active factors.